JEWELRY
MAKING

JEWELRY

MAKING

TIPS AND TRICKS
OF THE TRADE

STEPHEN O'KEEFFE

 **krause publications**
An F&W Publications Company

700 East State Street • Iola, WI 54990-0001
715-445-2214 • 888-457-2873
www.krause.com

A QUARTO BOOK

First published in North America in 2003
by Krause Publications, 700 East State Street
Iola, WI 54990-0001

Library of Congress Catalog Card No 2003105285

ISBN 0-87349-650-7

QUAR.HCJM

Conceived, designed, and produced by
Quarto Publishing plc
The Old Brewery
6 Blundell Street
London N7 9BH

Senior project editor **Nadia Naqib**
Senior art editor **Sally Bond**
Designer **Jill Mumford**
Text editors **Claire Waite-Brown**
Geraldine Christy
Illustrator **John Woodcock**
Photographer **Colin Bowling**
Indexer **Pamela Ellis**

Art director **Moira Clinch**
Publisher **Piers Spence**

Manufactured by Universal Graphics, Singapore
Printed by Leefung-Asco Printers Ltd, China

CONTENTS

FOREWORD

The jewelry maker is twice blessed. The rewards and satisfaction gained from the creative process are enhanced by the pleasure the finished products bring to others. Jewelry is unique in its sentimental value as the personal nature and the symbolism associated with it give the jewelry maker opportunities denied to other craftspeople.

Some years ago our daughter was married. She asked me to make her a gilded tiara, and of course I made the wedding rings. The rings were hallmarked. The tiny pieces of gold that had been scraped off for analysis were returned by the assay office with the rings. As the rings were made of 22-carat gold, it was possible for me to tease them out into flat strips. I then rearranged the tiny pieces of gold and soldered them to a piece of silver in the form of a cross. The wedding took place on a glorious summer's day. The sun shone down on the brilliant golden tiara and the little cross, and the story of its making was received with tears of joy.

I have in my desk drawer two pieces of silver jewelry. These were made by my father long before I was born. I sometimes show them to my students as good examples of the art of repoussé. When my grandchildren wear this jewelry, a connection is made between the wearer and the long dead craftsman.

This pendant is made of mother of pearl set in a silver mount with silver wire balls and repoussé leaves. This is the work of the author's father, Stephen O'Keeffe.

This silver buckle with a fish design was made in repoussé. The work of the author's father, Stephen O'Keeffe.

This running hound brooch is also modeled in repoussé of silver. This is the work of the author's father, Stephen O'Keeffe.

In pursuing the craft of jewelry making we are following in the footsteps of countless generations of craftspeople. The jewelers of ancient Egypt would probably recognize much of the equipment used by the craftspeople of today. It is well that we keep this in mind for an appreciation of the work of the ancients and some knowledge of how they made their jewelry enhances the enjoyment we derive from our own work.

The modern craftsperson has a bewildering array of tools at his or her disposal and jewelry materials are available in every conceivable form. In spite of this, however, there are still stages in the making of jewelry that are real stumbling blocks. The jeweler does not exist who has not accidentally melted his or her work at a crucial stage or tangled a near-finished piece in a polishing machine. This book is about how to attain success by concentrating on the simple aspects of jewelry making and by finding alternative ways of doing the difficult things, and, if possible, of avoiding them altogether.

This little silver cross was embellished with gold, as a gift to the bride.

The bride's gilded tiara. This is made in copper wire sections, soldered together, then gold plated.

The genius seldom makes a good teacher. If you find something easy to learn you will probably find it hard to teach. The difficulties I have encountered in jewelry making inform much of the content of this book.

GETTING STARTED

Getting started in jewelry making can be costly. Many jewelry tools are designed specifically for the working of precious metals and are consequently expensive. In this section some cost-cutting suggestions are made, and the making of some simple but useful tools demonstrated.

When buying tools for jewelry making you should buy the best you can afford. There are of course limits to one's budget, and money saved on some tools can be wisely spent on other better-quality ones. Never economize on shears and cutters. The cheaper ones are often made of inferior steel and a cutting tool that does not hold an edge is close to useless. Look out for older secondhand tools as these are often superior in quality to the equivalent new items.

It is very easy for the beginner to spend unwisely. As you gain experience and become more certain of your needs and of your continuing commitment to the craft, you can replace your homemade or cheaply acquired tools with greater confidence.

THE ACQUISITION OF TOOLS

THE WORK BENCH

The first requirement of a jewelry maker is a solid bench or table. The top of the bench should be about mid-chest height for a comfortable working posture, so make it a high table or a low chair.

The bench peg is a vital piece of equipment and will become your most useful tool. It can be screwed down permanently or fixed to the table with a clamp. Use your peg as your main supporting tool for holding metal steady while sawing and filing. The version shown here has a range of holes and slots for filing the ends of wires and strips of metal. The slot through the middle is used to accommodate a piercing saw. The bench peg, which is made of a close-grained wood such as maple, can and should be constantly modified by sawing, filing, and drilling to suit the work in hand.

G-clamp

Bench peg

Permanent pen

Try square

soft pencil

Center punch

Carpenter's tape
(tape measure)

Dividers

scriber

Ruler

MARKING TOOLS

For measuring, a 6-inch (150-mm) plastic rule will serve most needs. A carpenter's tape measure is the most convenient tool for longer measurements. A center punch is used with a hammer to mark holes for drilling. A fine permanent pen, a soft pencil, and a scriber are also useful marking tools. Use a small try square to mark lines at right angles to an edge, and a pair of dividers to scribe lines parallel to an edge. Dividers are also used for scribing arcs and circles.

CUTTERS

Jeweler's shears should be purchased first as these can cut most things. However they are ideally suited to cutting thin sheet metal. To cut thicker metal, heavy-duty shears such as gilbows are required. End- or side-cutters are used to cut wire. Side cutters can be used to cut thick wire as a large force can be applied to the bottom of the jaws nearest the fulcrum. The piercing saw is used for cutting complex shapes and internal curves in sheet metal, and for making jump rings. Buy a selection of blades for the saw. A junior hacksaw is good for sawing wood and metal. A coping saw has a thicker blade than a piercing saw and can be more effective on wood or acrylic.

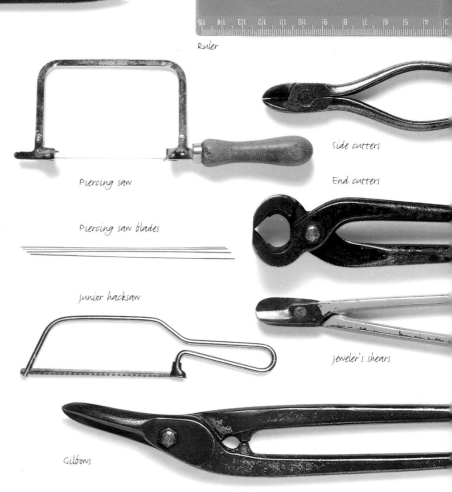

Piercing saw

Side cutters

End cutters

Piercing saw blades

Junior hacksaw

Jeweler's shears

Gilbows

FILES

Files are available in different shapes and sizes and are graded according to how coarse or fine they are. Buy a 6-inch (150-mm) smooth-cut hand file to start with. Hand files are flat on both sides, with one completely smooth or "safe" edge, and will serve most purposes. A half-round file will also be useful; this can be 4 inches (100 mm) and smooth-cut like the hand file. Needle files are used for intricate work and are available in a range of shapes. The round, parallel files used to sharpen chain saws are also of value to the jewelry maker.

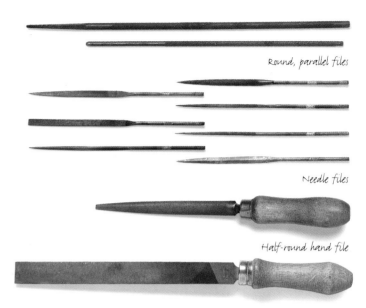

Round, parallel files

Needle files

Half-round hand file

Straight hand file

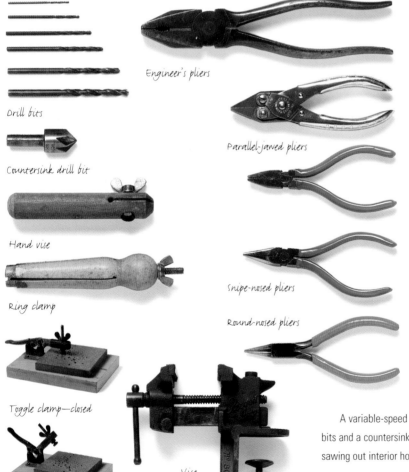

Drill bits

Countersink drill bit

Hand vise

Ring clamp

Toggle clamp—closed

Toggle clamp—open

Engineer's pliers

Parallel-jawed pliers

Snipe-nosed pliers

Round-nosed pliers

Vise

HOLDING DEVICES

If you have a strong vise bolted to your bench, you can use it for holding wire, steel rods, or other tools. Clamp a small vise with 2-inch (50-mm) jaws to the edge of the work bench or table. A hand vise is also useful and you can make one from a short piece of broom handle. A ring clamp is almost indispensable, particularly when setting cabochons. The toggle clamp is used for holding work to be drilled and should be screwed to a piece of plywood.

You will need several pairs of pliers—parallel-jawed pliers and round-nosed pliers to begin with, and a pair of pointed or snipe-nosed pliers as you progress in the craft. Jeweler's pliers have smooth jaws to prevent damage to soft metal. Engineer's pliers, which have serrated jaws, are used to achieve a secure grip, particularly when wire drawing.

A variable-speed electric hand-drill together with a set of drill bits and a countersink drill are also indispensable, particularly for sawing out interior holes in metal.

SOLDERING EQUIPMENT

Perhaps the most important jewelry-making tool is the soldering torch. A large version is used mainly by plumbers, while a smaller-sized torch is used by cooks. If you are going to buy one torch, it is best to buy the larger one as this can be used for any of the projects in this book. To complete your soldering kit you will need a firebrick or a piece of charcoal, a borax cone (flux) and a piece of slate, a pair of tweezers with a locking ring, and a small paintbrush. You will also need a heatproof glass or ceramic acid jar in which to hold acid pickle. The pickle is used to clean off residual flux after soldering. Acid pickle commonly consists of a one-to-five ratio of sulfuric acid in water. Always add the acid to cold water a little at a time as heat is generated as a result. Never add water to acid; always add acid to water.

Soldering torch

Piece of slate

Borax cone

Firebrick

Charcoal block

Piece of slate

Tweezers with locking ring

small paintbrush

Cook's torch

Acid solution

HAMMERS AND MALLETS

If you only have one hammer to begin with, make it a ball-peen hammer. This has a flat face on one side and a domed one on the other, both of which must be kept highly polished. A cross-peen hammer can have its flat face left rough for use with punches. The flat face of a ball-peen or cross-peen hammer is used for planishing. The jewelry maker's mallet is usually made of rolled hide but a wooden one will also suffice.

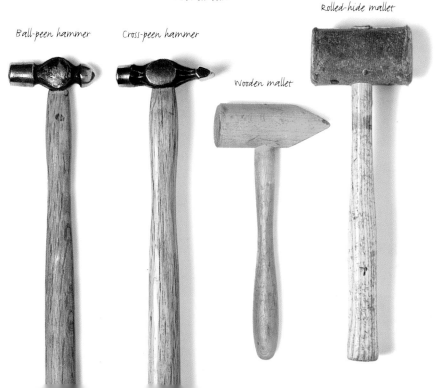

Ball-peen hammer

Cross-peen hammer

Wooden mallet

Rolled-hide mallet

OTHER EQUIPMENT

TAPERED MANDRELS AND STAKES

A selection of tapered mandrels is an essential part of the jewelry maker's equipment. Start with a ring mandrel which tapers from about 1 inch (25 mm) in diameter to about ²⁵⁄₆₄ in (10 mm). Thinner mandrels are used in the making of settings for stones. Aim to collect various objects, such as rolling pins and table legs to use as mandrels. At least two stakes, one flat and the other domed, will be needed for hammering on.

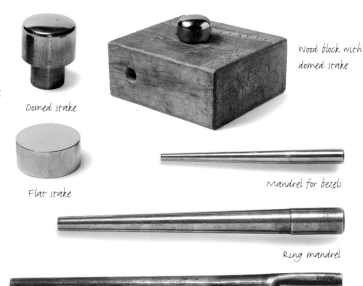

Domed stake

Wood block with domed stake

Flat stake

Mandrel for bezels

Ring mandrel

ROLLING MILL

The rolling mill is used to roll sheet metal to a precise thickness. It can also be used to create a pattern or texture on your work.

Mandrel made from bicycle part

SWAGE BLOCK

A swage block in conjunction with a steel rod and hammer is used to shape flat strips of metal into fine pieces of tubing. You can make a swage block by sawing down a series of holes in a hardwood block.

DRAWPLATES

Drawplates are used to draw down wire to a thinner dimension. If you can afford only one draw-plate, make it a plate with round holes in it.

Steel swage block

Wooden swage block

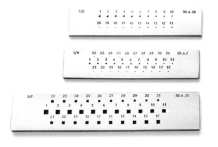

Drawplates

Rolling mill

DOMING BLOCK

A doming block and a set of punches are useful for shaping hollow metal discs. Brass blocks are cheaper than steel ones and will last as long provided you use wooden punches with them.

METAL PUNCHES

Metal punches with chamfers (slants or inclinations of their top surface) are invaluable for fitting linings into rings.

Doming block

Metal punches

Wooden punch

PUSHER AND BURNISHER

The pusher and burnisher are used in the setting of cabochons.

Pusher

Burnisher

BENDING JIG

A bending jig is used to bend wire into patterns. (See pages 80–81 to find out how you can make your own jig, and pages 82–83 to see how you can use a jig to make jewelry items.)

Bending Jig

POLISHING EQUIPMENT

Although not essential, a polishing machine is a very useful item of equipment that can save you a great deal of time. Two polishing mops are required for each grade of polish used, one for applying the polish and the other for cleaning off the residue left by the first mop.

Tripoli is a general-purpose polish and rouge, which can be bought in block or powdered form. It imparts a high polish to metal work. Jeweler's rouge is finer than tripoli and is often the last polish to be used in the polishing process. There are polishing compounds designed specifically for polishing acrylic. Only one mop is needed for acrylic polishes as they produces a powdery residue that can be wiped away with a cloth.

You can make a collection of polishing sticks using strips of plywood and dowel covered with emery paper and suede or leather. A selection of strings and pieces of tape can be coated with polish and used to polish the insides of holes and other awkward places. A smooth soft stone such as water of Ayr stone or slate can be filed to shape, and used with water to smooth awkward places prior to polishing.

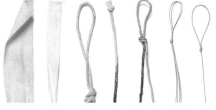

Strings/tape for polishing

Polishing sticks

Polishing strip (suede)

Piece of slate

Ring polishing stick with and without ring

Polishes

soft cloth

Polishing machine

Mop and acrylic polish

REPOUSSÉ TOOLS

To begin repoussé, you will need a block of wood about 4¾ in (120 mm) square. This must have a uniform grain; sycamore or maple are ideal, but most softwoods are suitable, too. Use the end grain for repoussé and the sides for drilling on or matting. A good collection of repoussé punches can run to twenty or thirty but a start can be made with seven or eight. A lining or tracing punch can be made from an old screwdriver blade. One or two blocking punches will be needed for pushing up areas from the back of the work, and one or two matting punches for the creation of texture, usually as background to the main design. The little cross punches shown here are made from jeweler's screwdrivers. The circle punches can be made by drilling the ends of round bars with a center drill. Like all repoussé punches they must be rounded off and polished. Ball bearings of different sizes, iron binding wire, and a steel rod with beveled ends are also useful repoussé tools. A repoussé hammer has a broad face and flexible shaft, suitable for use with punches.

Repoussé hammer

Cross section of circle punch

Circle punches

Curved lining punch

Tracing (lining) punches

Iron binding wire

Ball bearings

Cross punches

Matting punch

Blocking punches

THE MAKING OF SPECIALIST TOOLS

Not everyone will have the means, either in terms of equipment or expertise, to make all the tools shown here. Most of the projects described in this book are possible to make without their use. However if you are serious about jewelry making and would like to design tools that are specific to your needs, it is well worth investing the time and effort in making some of your own tools.

SIZING RINGS

All these rings have the length of metal used engraved on them (for example, $2\frac{23}{64}$, $2\frac{19}{32}$, and $2\frac{45}{64}$ in [64, 66, and 68 mm]). Use them with standard ring gauges and a ring mandrel to estimate the length of ring bands (ring blanks). They are especially useful for fitting linings into rings.

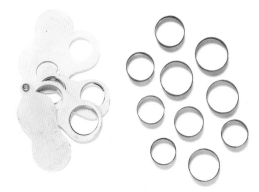

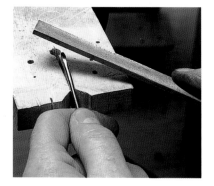

FLATTENING DEVICE

This simple tool is made from two pieces of 2 in (50 mm) mild steel bar, faced off in a lathe to make them perfectly flat and square. The plastic tube, into which the bars are a sliding fit, ensures that the faces come together square to each other and also acts as a guard against trapped fingers. The handle is made from $\frac{25}{64}$ in (10 mm) mild steel bar, threaded and screwed into a hole in one of the bars.

BURNISHER

This little tool is used for making adjustments to scrolls. Round off the end of an electrician's screwdriver with a file and emery paper, then polish.

Handmade burnisher

DISC SANDING MACHINE

A sanding machine is invaluable for smoothing and abrading acrylic. The machine shown here was made using an old washing machine motor. The plywood disc is screwed onto one of the pulleys from the machine, which is in turn fixed directly to the motor spindle. How you fasten the motor to the base will depend on its mountings as not all motors are suitable for this purpose. The wooden table must be square to the disc and removable for the replacement of abrasive discs. Ask a qualified electrician to check your wiring before you use the machine.

STRIP BENDING PLIERS

This device can be used for bending strips of thin metal that are too wide to bend accurately using round-nosed pliers. Any radius can be formed simply by threading a short length of tubing onto the removable spindle. The device is shown in use on page 114.

YOU WILL NEED
- Block of hardwood, 6 x 1⅜ x 1³⁄₁₆ in) 150 x 35 x 30 mm)
- Electric drill and ¹⁹⁄₆₄ in (7.5 mm), ⁵⁄₃₂ in (4 mm), and ³⁄₃₂ in (2.5 mm) drill bits
- Small wood saw
- Disc sanding machine
- 1³⁄₁₆ in (30 mm) x ⁵⁄₃₂ in (4 mm) nut and bolt
- Vise
- ³⁄₃₂ in (2.5 mm) rod or wire for spindle
- ¹⁹⁄₃₂ in (15 mm) length of ¹⁵⁄₃₂ in (12 mm) dowel
- Two panel pins
- Ball-peen hammer
- Wood glue

1 Mark out the shape and the position of the two holes on the block of wood. Drill the smaller hole using the ³⁄₃₂ in (2.5 mm) drill bit and the larger hole using the ⁵⁄₃₂ in (4 mm) bit.

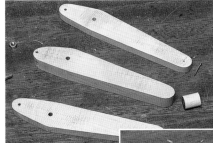

Cross section of wood showing larger hole.

2 Saw out the shape and finish it with a sanding machine. Drill both sides of the ⁵⁄₃₂ in (4 mm) hole with the ¹⁹⁄₆₄ in (7.5 mm) drill to receive the bolt head on one side, and the nut on the other.

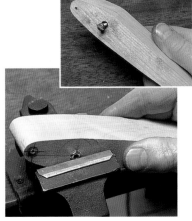

3 Squeeze the nut into place in the vise.

4 Use the wood saw to slice the wood into three pieces. Turn the center section upside down and assemble the pieces by screwing the ⁵⁄₃₂ in (4 mm) bolt into the captive nut.

5 Fix the ³⁄₃₂ in (2.5 mm) spindle in place between the two holes of the same diameter. Glue and pin the short dowel into place at the handle end.

6 The spindle around which the strip of silver is bent is ³⁄₃₂ in (2.5 mm) steel. You could use a thinner spindle in the same holes as it does not need to be a tight fit.

METALS

With the exception of gold and platinum, the metals used in jewelry making are surprisingly inexpensive. The scale of most projects is small and much use can be made of recycled material such as cutlery and copper electrical wire. Sterling silver's relatively low melting point of about 1562°F (850°C) makes it vulnerable during soldering—when heated to soldering temperature, it is prone to fire stain, which is a thin layer of oxide that must be removed with abrasives before polishing is carried out. Silver is used in both sheet and wire form. The wire used is round, and all round-wire measurements in this book are given in the form of length by diameter (for example, 4 x ½ in [100 x 1 mm]). Copper is invaluable as a component of most of the metals used by the jewelry maker. It is easily worked, can be etched, and its high melting point (1981°F [1083°C] makes it difficult to melt during soldering. Gilding metal is an alloy of copper and zinc. Its color most resembles gold, it is easy to work, and it etches well. Brass is also an alloy of copper and zinc and is usually yellow in color. Brass, copper, and gilding metal can all be bought in sheet or wire form. Bronze is an alloy of copper and tin; the modern alloy also contains some zinc. Bronze, which is used in sheet form, tarnishes to a dark brown color with age. Nickel silver contains very little nickel and no silver as copper is its main component. It etches well using ferric chloride as the etchant. Old cutlery is a good, inexpensive source of nickel silver. Pewter is an alloy of tin, antimony, and copper. Its low melting point makes it ideal for casting.

Various thicknesses of silver wire

Various thicknesses of copper and brass wire and gilding metal.

silver sheet

Gilding metal sheet

Brass sheet

Bronze sheet

silver bearer wire (for setting stones)

DESIGNING

Designing is never easy. To imagine a thing in the mind's eye, to draw it, make a model of it, and then to make a realistic plan for making it is probably the most difficult part of jewelry making. You may find some of the strategies suggested here, helpful. The design process is considered as a practical problem-solving activity, not directly concerned with matters of taste or aesthetics, although any well-made object that functions as intended will probably be pleasing to the eye. Designing can take many forms and call upon varied skills such as observing, collecting, selecting, analyzing, drawing, modeling, and planning. Find a route that suits you and be receptive to change and adaptation. Perhaps the most important requirement for successful jewelry design is a familiarity with the basic techniques of jewelry making. There is little point in designing something, however wonderful, if it requires the skills of a professional to make it. Gain experience by copying other people's designs before making your own.

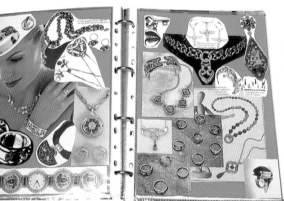

KEEPING A SCRAPBOOK

The first stage of the design process involves deciding what you are going to make. This is not always as straightforward as you may think. A scrapbook can be useful at this stage. Pictures and designs you encounter in magazines, catalogs, and books should be stored away for future reference. Photographs of professionally made jewelry pieces are a very useful source of inspiration.

Your collection need not be restricted to images of jewelry. Graphic designs and work in wrought iron, for example, can provide ideas, as can company logos, heraldic devices, and wallpaper patterns. Consider religious and other cultural symbols, the zodiac, and Japanese birth signs. Monograms, lines of poetry, and quotations can be used to make a design appropriate to an individual. Names, dates, and prose take on an added dimension when realized in precious metal.

KEEPING A DESIGN JOURNAL

As well as a scrapbook, a journal is useful for recording sketches and ideas. A loose-leaf format is ideal for a design journal as it means you can add, discard, or rearrange the pages. The format also encourages you to include sketches and ideas that you would perhaps be reluctant to record in a hardback sketchbook. Use your design journal to include accounts of projects you have made, with notes and sketches and lists of materials used.

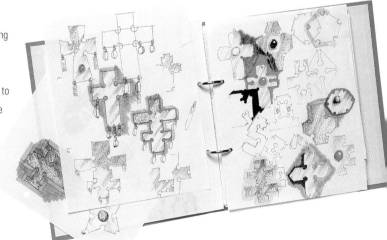

DESIGN SHEETS

Once you have decided what you are going to make, try to impose some constraints. For example, you may decide to make a necklace composed of five three-sided forms connected with jump rings and to use the technique of repoussé to shape the forms.

Once you have decided on a basic concept, draw up a design sheet to allow you to explore all possible designs (see example, left). As your sheet fills up, you will find that your ideas feed on each other and multiply. A good design sheet takes time and effort and can be a satisfying end in itself. Use color sparingly to represent different metals. The finished design sheet should of course be filed away in your design journal for future reference.

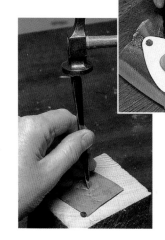

MAKING MODELS

Having chosen your main design, you can now make a model of it in copper. This affords you the chance to tackle any difficulties in the making of the piece before you use a valuable piece of silver. The finished model will also allow you to make a realistic assessment of how your design looks in practice.

Modeling is an important part of the design process and can often replace drawing as a means of forming ideas. In the case of repoussé you can make models using a ballpoint pen and beer cans. String is a useful modeling material, particularly for designing knot jewelry. Card can be used in place of sheet metal and even clay or plasticine can be used to practice making designs. Making scrolls or rings using copper wire or string can be far more effective than drawing in creating designs.

TEMPLATES

Templates and jigs can be a valuable design resource and may amply repay the time and effort spent on making them. Circle and ellipse templates can be bought and other shapes made out of thin card.

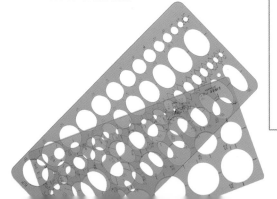

POINTS TO NOTE

When evaluating your designs and finished pieces, you must consider the following:

- Has the relevant material been used to good effect? This is an important consideration where precious metal is concerned.
- Is the object safe to use, with no sharp edges or points?
- Is it comfortable to wear?
- Do any catches, pins, or hooks keep the item secure?
- Is the item easy to clean and polish?
- What would you do differently if you had to make the piece again?

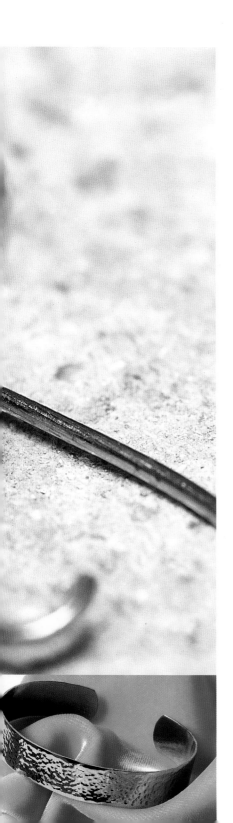

CHAPTER 1

BASIC TECHNIQUES and PROJECTS

The basic techniques of jewelry making, as with most crafts involving the use of resistant material, are cutting, forming, and joining. Cutting uses shears, saws, drills, files, and abrasives. Forming requires mallets, hammers, stakes, mandrels, and pliers, while joining employs silver solder.

This chapter covers the more commonly used basic techniques; other more specialized means of cutting, forming, and joining are described in the next chapter. Finishing techniques involving abrading and polishing are also described in this chapter.

We learn by doing! Most of these techniques are demonstrated in the context of simple projects, mainly using base metals such as brass or bronze. These same techniques can then be applied to silver or gold. Always practice on base metals first before turning to precious metals to make your final jewelry piece.

LESSON: **CUTTING**

CUTTING WITH SHEARS

The most convenient way to cut metal is with jeweler's shears. There is usually some distortion of the sheared edge, but subsequent filing (see page 25) and planishing (see page 28) should remove this problem altogether. You can use jeweler's shears to cut thin metal, but you will probably need a heavier tool such as gilbows (heavy shears) to cut anything thicker than ⅟₃₂ in (1 mm). Annealing the metal (see page 30) will make cutting it with shears easier.

YOU WILL NEED

- Bench peg and vise
- Gilbows or similar
- Hook bolts
- Annealed sheet metal (see page 30)
- Scriber
- Try square
- Jewler's shears
- Dividers
- Copper wire
- End or side cutters
- Piercing saw and blade
- Electric drill
- Plywood or hard board (for very thin metal and double-sided tape)
- Hand file
- Emery boards of varying grades

CUTTING WITH GILBOWS

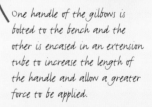

Hold one handle of the gilbows in a vise or bolt it to the bench with hook bolts as shown right. This makes it much easier to apply the necessary force—a downward force is easier to apply than a one-handed squeezing force (as above).

One handle of the gilbows is bolted to the bench and the other is encased in an extension tube to increase the length of the handle and allow a greater force to be applied.

CUTTING WITH JEWELER'S SHEARS

1 To cut off a strip of metal, first scribe a line using a scriber and a try square—this will be the datum edge. Trim the edge straight and square using jeweler's shears.

2 Mark out the strip with dividers set to the required width. Be sure to keep the non-scribing point of the dividers pressed firmly against the edge of the metal. Then use the shears to cut along the scribed line. File the edges (see page 25).

CUTTING A CURVED EDGE

To cut out a curved edge with shears, first cut out the shape oversized to within 1⁄32 in (1 mm) or so of the scribed line using straight-line cuts. As you cut to the line, the thin strip that remains will bend easily away from the shears. File the edges (see page 25).

CUTTING WIRE

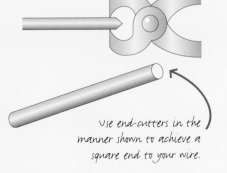

Use end-cutters in the manner shown to achieve a square end to your wire.

Shears can also be used to cut wire, but end- (above) or side-cutters (top) are more suitable. Cut the wire slightly oversized and trim it back to leave both ends square.

CUTTING WITH A PIERCING SAW

When a neater edge or an internal curve is needed on sheet metal, use a piercing saw. This type of saw has fine, sharp teeth, so little force is required to use one effectively. The keys to success with this tool are to choose the correct blade, to have the blade tensioned correctly, and to keep a very relaxed grip on the handle. A block of beeswax is used as a lubricant by either rubbing it against the teeth or by warming the metal to be cut then rubbing the wax over its surface to create a thin film.

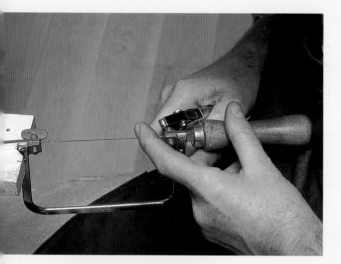

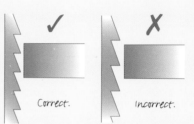

Correct.   Incorrect.

Choose a blade that is fine enough for two or more teeth to be in contact with the edge of the metal.

1 To insert the blade in the saw frame, hold the front end of the frame against the bench peg and support the handle against your chest. Fix the blade into the front end of the frame, with the teeth pointing toward the handle then squeeze the frame slightly to press the blade into the fixing clamp at the handle end by about ⅛ in (3 mm). This will provide the required tension in the blade.

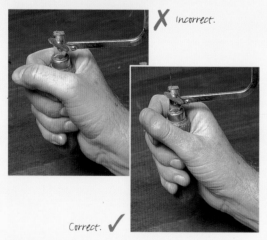

✗ Incorrect.

Correct. ✓

2 Always hold the saw at a 90-degree angle to your work. Hold the handle with just enough pressure to prevent it slipping through the fingers. Too firm a grip will invariably lead to the blade breaking.

3 Support the work on the bench peg, with your free hand applying firm downward pressure on the work. Gradually move both work and saw, avoiding sudden twists as you follow the line. To prevent the blade from snagging at the start of a cut, apply it to the edge of the metal sideways, and gradually move it around once a start has been made.

4 Try to use as much of the blade as possible. Short strokes wear the blade out over part of its length and lead to jamming when the unworn section enters the narrower saw-cut made by the worn section. To cut out an internal shape, first make a hole in the metal with a drill (see page 26) then thread the blade through the hole before fastening it into the frame.

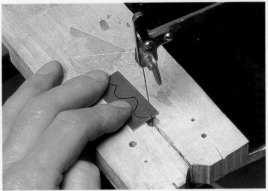

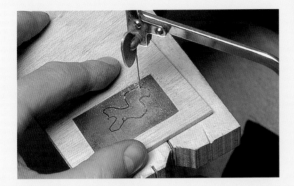

5 When sawing very thin metal it is a good idea to fix it to a piece of plywood or hardboard with double-sided tape. This helps to prevent the blade from snagging on the thin metal.

FINISHING

1 Edges sawn with a piercing saw require very little finishing, and you can finish sheared edges with a file and emery boards. To work on the sides, hold the metal in a vise using vise guards. Support the file at both ends and move it over the metal at an angle of about 45 degrees.

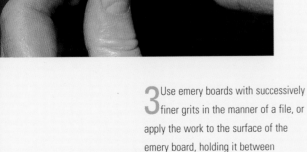

2 File the ends with the work held in the groove at the front of the bench peg. Press the file flat against the surface of the wood to file the ends square.

3 Use emery boards with successively finer grits in the manner of a file, or apply the work to the surface of the emery board, holding it between your finger and thumb.

LESSON: DRILLING

Hole drilling is a necessary part of jewelry making, whether for hanging or for decorative purposes. An open section in the center of a sheet of metal can be achieved by drilling a small hole in the center and threading a piercing saw blade through it. Before drilling the hole it is necessary to make a small indent with a center punch. This provides a starting point for the drill and prevents it from sliding over the metal surface. Drill bits, like saw blades, are available in a variety of different sizes and can be used in many different types of drill.

YOU WILL NEED
- Sheet metal
- Dividers
- Center punch
- Hammer
- Steel plate
- Electric drill and two bits, one larger than the required hole size
- Vise or toggle clamp
- Wood block

Hole positions for drilling.

1 Mark the position of each hole, using dividers to make a cross into which to slide the point of the center punch.

2 Place the work on a plain piece of steel, not a polished stake. Strike the punch with a hammer just once. If the indent is not deep enough, replace the punch carefully and strike it a second time; this will prevent a double mark occurring should the punch bounce out of place.

3 Hold the work to be drilled securely against a smooth piece of wood, either in a vise or a toggle clamp (as left)—metal breaking loose during drilling can be dangerous. The wood will reduce the formation of a burr on the back of the hole.

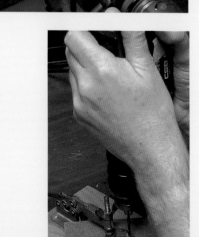

4 Use a portable electric drill on a slow speed with the power locked on. Then use both hands to ensure that the drill is held at right angles to the surface of the metal throughout the process. This is most important as any tilting will result in the drill jamming and probably a breakage.

5 Remove the burr with a larger drill bit held in the fingers, having first ground off the bit's edge to prevent it biting into the metal. A file would scratch the surface of the metal surrounding the hole. Holes larger than $^{15}/_{64}$ in (6 mm) should be drilled through a smaller hole called a pilot hole.

LESSON: FORMING

There is almost no limit to the ways in which metal can be formed. The softer non-ferrous metals used in jewelry making are particularly easy to form. Wire can be drawn down and changed in section using drawplates, and sheet metal can be changed out of all recognition by means of hammers and formers. A former is a tool around which metal is formed, be it a stake, a mandrel, or a swage or doming block. This lesson covers the basic techniques of forming. Other more specialized forming techniques, such as planishing and wire drawing are covered elsewhere in the book.

YOU WILL NEED
- Rolled-hide mallet
- Wood or metal block
- Ring mandrel
- Doming block
- Wooden doming punch
- Ball-peen hammer

FLATTENING

To flatten a piece of metal, use a rolled-hide mallet on a flat surface of wood or metal. Turn the piece to work on it from either end and from both sides; this will help to even out the bumps.

FORMING A RING

A ring formed on a tapered mandrel will become round, but it will remain the same size and you can preserve any pattern on it by using a rolled-hide mallet. Twist the ring so that you can use the mallet to tap down any bumps. Pull it down the mandrel as it becomes more nearly round.

DOMING

Use wooden punches and the flat face of a ball-peen hammer with a doming block if you wish a piece of flat metal to become domed. Move the piece around in the hollow to allow the punch to cover all of the surface while remaining upright.

LESSON: PLANISHING

Planishing is the process of flattening sheet metal using a planishing hammer. When polished, the planished surface reflects light in a livelier way and the object in question is better able to withstand the slight scratches that would otherwise show clearly on a mirrored surface. Planishing can also be used to impart surface texture to metal.

YOU WILL NEED
- Planishing hammers
- Stake
- Sheet metal
- Rolling mill

USING PLANISHING HAMMERS

Position the stake at about elbow height.

Position a stake over a bench or table leg, at about elbow height, and position the work on the stake. This will allow you to bring your hammer down square to the work without the need to reach forward. Most people prefer to stand when planishing. You should aim to planish the whole surface with hammer blows delivered as evenly as possible.

You can also planish a piece of work on a mandrel. This broad ring has been planished using a cross-peen hammer to create a bark-like effect.

Various patterns can be created with just two or three hammers.

USING A ROLLING MILL

1 The rolling mill reduces the thickness of a sheet of metal as the sheet is passed through it. The "T" handle on the top is used to adjust the gap between the rollers. As the long handle is turned, the rollers pull the metal between them, compressing it slightly with each pass.

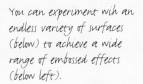

2 You can also use a rolling mill to create patterns on metal. With the two rollers tightened to the precise thickness of the metal sheet, most material will make an imprint on it. Lace curtain material is particularly effective, and even hair will make a significant impression on an annealed silver sheet.

Here, aida, an evenly woven fabric with regularly spaced holes, was used to create a textured effect on silver.

You can experiment with an endless variety of surfaces (below) to achieve a wide range of embossed effects (below left).

LESSON: ANNEALING

Most people when asked to break a piece of metal without the use of tools do so by bending it back and forth repeatedly. This invariably results in the metal being broken. This is because when metal is bent, stretched, hammered, or otherwise deformed, it becomes harder and therefore brittle. This effect is called "work hardening." Annealing is the process of heating metal to prevent it from cracking and make it easier to work. A subdued light is necessary for annealing for the color change to be easily seen.

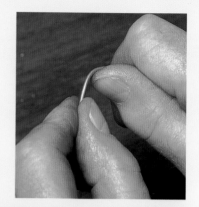

YOU WILL NEED
- Cookie tin
- Firebrick
- Sheet metal
- Wire
- Soldering torch

A cookie tin on end will shade the light quite well. Lean sheet metal against a firebrick where it will heat up more quickly than if it is laid flat on the ground because the firebrick reflects heat back onto the metal. Fine wire melts easily so is best annealed carefully in mid-air, away from heat-reflecting firebricks. Use a soldering torch to heat the metal evenly with a soft flame.

To heat the metal, lean it against a fire-brick rather than laying it flat.

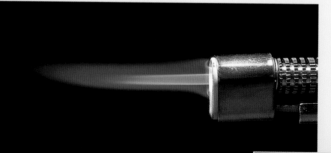

The flame with less air in it is called a reducing flame.

THE ANNEALING FLAME

The annealing flame is softer than that used for soldering and is therefore less likely to oxidize the metal. The color of the metal at annealing temperature is dull red, at which point it is fully softened—any hotter and the structure of the metal could be damaged.

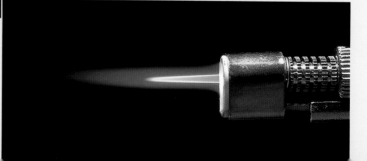

This oxidizing flame is too hot for annealing.

LESSON: SOLDERING

Soldering is the process of joining metals using heat and silver-based alloys or "solders," which, when heated to a certain temperature, create the join. Careful preparation and attention to detail are vital in soldering, particularly at the beginning of the process because once the operation goes wrong, it is very difficult to correct.

The first requirement in soldering is that the metals to be joined should fit together perfectly with no gaps or burrs. The metal around the join must then be cleaned free of any grease or oxide, either with a scraper or with emery paper. Soldering flux in the form of borax prevents the formation of oxide during heating and allows the molten solder to flow. Flux should be applied to the metal after it has been cleaned of oxide. Solder is then placed carefully in place at the join and heat is applied, gently at first, then more vigorously, until the solder melts and flows around the join. Solder is graded by melting point and the five main types are extra easy (with the lowest melting point), easy, medium, hard, and enameling. Only easy and hard solder are used for the projects in this book.

YOU WILL NEED

- Emery paper
- Slate or dish
- Borax cone
- Fine paintbrush
- Jeweler's shears
- Strip of solder
- Pair of tweezers
- Soldering torch
- Firebricks
- Iron or copper rods
- Tripod
- Acid solution in jar
- Retrieving hook
- Water for cooling and mixing

PREPARING THE JOIN

1 Use emery paper to clean the join. Mix the flux by grinding a borax cone on a slate or dish with some water. Use a fine paintbrush to paint the flux onto the join.

The flux mixture should have the consistency of milk.

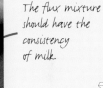

2 Use jeweler's shears to cut pallions of approximately ½₂ in (1 mm) square from a strip of solder.

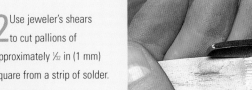

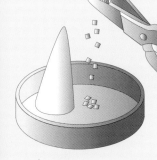

Use shears to cut pallions of solder.

3 Using tweezers, place the pallions of solder across the join. First, heat the work gently, away from the join. Then concentrate the heat on the join, ensuring both sides get equally hot. As soon as the solder flows, withdraw the heat.

Ensure that the pallions touch both sides of the metal.

SOLDERING A BROAD BAND

1 When a broad band is to be soldered, particularly one with a pattern, it is better to place the solder on the band's inside, because residual solidified solder may later have to be filed off. Raise the band out of direct contact with the firebrick using iron or copper wire. This will allow the molten solder to flow evenly around the join.

2 Since heavy metal takes longer to reach soldering temperature than lighter metal or wire, place another piece of firebrick behind the work to reflect the heat onto the metal. Heat the whole band first before heating the join. The metal must be heated quickly, because the soldering flux will deteriorate if heated for too long, and evenly, to prevent heat from the area to be soldered escaping to colder parts of the band.

SOLDERING METAL PIECES OF UNEQUAL SIZE

1 An important requirement in soldering is that both sides of the join reach soldering temperature at the same time, allowing the solder to flow equally to both sides. When soldering small pieces, such as wires or the settings for stones, onto larger pieces, heat them from beneath a tripod. This ensures that the larger component heats up before the smaller one. If heated from above the smaller part will overheat and might even melt long before the larger one is hot enough.

2 Dip the smaller piece in the flux and then place it on the base plate, making an imprint.

3 Place the pallions of solder onto the line left by the smaller piece, and place the wire over them. This is a delicate operation and may take several attempts before all is in place, but patience is rewarded when the solder flows just where it is needed.

SOLDERING METAL DOMES

To solder metal domes together, drop the domes face down into the flux. Sandwich them with pallions of solder and heat them.

POINTS TO NOTE

- The application of flux is important—if oxide film is allowed to build up on the join it will be impossible to solder.
- Flux has a limited life. At the high temperatures of molten metal it soon deteriorates to a point where it is no longer effective.
- Too little flux applied to the join will degrade faster than the metal—too much will obscure the melting metal.
- Heating away from the join at first provides a kind of heat reservoir, which will reduce the time required for the fluxed area to reach melting temperature.
- It is important that the metal to be soldered reaches the required temperature before the solder does. If heat is directed onto the solder the pallion will ball up and may roll off to one side of the join before it flows.

Oxide film build up.

PICKLING

When the soldered metal has cooled, place it in the acid pickle—one part acid to five parts water—for five minutes to clean it. Iron will contaminate acid pickle. This means that all tweezers or hooks must be made of a non-ferrous metal such as copper.

LESSON: FINISHING TECHNIQUES

Finishing processes are perhaps the most important part of jewelry making and you may have to spend as much time on this stage as you spend on all the previous stages put together. A high polish is achieved by using a succession of abrasives, each one finer than the last. It is most important to keep abrasive polishes separate from each other and that you clean the work thoroughly after each stage. This prevents finer polishes from being contaminated by coarser ones.

Prevention is better than cure. While scratches can be removed by burnishing or scraping, try to avoid needless restoration by taking good care of all your tools. Examine them carefully before use—a speck of grit on a mallet or polishing device can do great damage.

Always have a soft cloth available on which to place your work in progress.

MACHINE POLISHING

Using a polishing machine is probably the easiest way to achieve a high polish on metal. Use the polishing mops in pairs—apply the polish with one and use the other to clean it off. Different mops—with a polish designed for steel—will be required for polishing hammers and stakes. You will need two wheels that are used with tripoli, a medium-grade polish, and two that are kept exclusively for use with jeweler's rouge, which is the finest of the available polishes and the last to be used in the polishing process.

The polishing compounds come in block form or as a powder. Tripoli is medium-grade, general-purpose polish. Rouge is the finest grade and is used to achieve a high polish.

POLISHING A RING

1 Hold the work against the bottom front quarter of the revolving wheel. Keep turning it constantly, always polishing away from the center and toward the trailing edge.

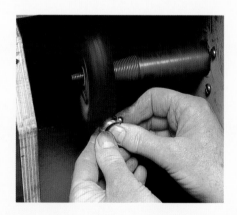

2 Keep a tight grip on work that you are polishing— the fast-moving wheel can easily pull work from your grasp with disastrous results. If you are polishing a ring, mount it on a ring holder or a piece of dowel.

YOU WILL NEED
- Bench peg and vise
- Polishing machine
- Wood blocks, plastic pipe, or wire to support the work
- Tripoli
- Polishing pad
- Jeweler's rouge
- Hand file
- Emery boards of varying grades
- Steel burnisher
- Old file, hacksaw blade, or penknife blade
- Water of Ayr stone
- String
- Soft pad

POLISHING WIRE

Support a thin strip of metal or a length of wire on a piece of wood or metal.

POLISHING A CHAIN OR THIN WIRE

Wrap thin wire or chain around something; a piece of plastic pipe or the head of a mallet are ideal.

POLISHING A POMANDER

An item such as a small pomander is difficult to keep hold of, so thread it onto a length of wire, and carefully fold the ends of the thread away from the mop.

SAFETY CONSIDERATIONS

- If you have long hair, tie it back so that it is well away from the machine and take extra care with apron strings, long sleeves, bracelets, or anything else that might get tangled in the polishing wheel.

POINTS TO NOTE

- A common mistake is to over polish—if you completely remove the marks left by previous work the piece can appear bland and lifeless. A highly polished surface is all the better when seen alongside a satin finish.
- Using a polishing machine is not the only way to achieve a high polish. Other means are sometimes more suitable and invariably safer.

POLISHING BY HAND

A felt pad sprinkled with powdered rouge is safer than the polishing machine for delicate items such as the scroll shown here. A scrap of carpet will serve the purpose if felt is not available.

EDGE POLISHING

DRAW FILING

1 To bring a filed edge to a high polish begin by draw filing. Hold the hand file at both ends and, keeping it horizontal, draw it back and forth at right angles along the edge of the work.

EMERY BOARDS

2 Use emery boards with successively finer grits in much the same way as the hand file. Remember to keep them square to the edge to avoid rounding off.

3 Small pieces should be held in the hand and rubbed on an emery board. To create a satin finish on your work, rub it on an emery board against a straight edge such as a steel rule.

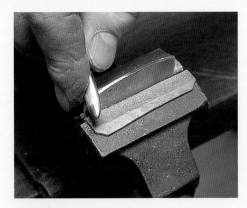

BURNISHING

4 Rub with a highly polished steel burnisher to bring the edge to a smooth finish. This will also harden the metal and retain the square, light-catching edge, which abrasive polishes sometimes fail to do.

POLISHING PAD

5 Finally, use a polishing pad with rouge to bring the edge to a high polish (see page 35).

REMOVING SCRATCHES

Remove scratches on the surface of metal with a scraper made from an old file or hacksaw blade—a penknife blade can be used as a scraper. Always scrape along the scratch, not across it. You can also use a burnisher to remove scratches in much the same way as the scraper. A burnisher works in a similar way to a planishing hammer, imparting a polish by rubbing the hard, polished metal over the surface of the softer metal. Burnishing (see page 36) is often the only means of hardening work after soldering.

USEFUL POLISHING TECHNIQUES

Water of Ayr stones.

WATER OF AYR STONE

Another means of finishing metal is to use "water of Ayr stone." This natural stone can be filed into shapes to reach awkward corners and is used with water to produce a pre-polish surface.

POLISH-COATED STRING

Lengths of string coated with polish are also useful. Secure one end to the bench, then thread awkward items onto one or more strands and rub them back and forth along the tightly held string.

VISE AND SOFT PAD

An alternative method of polishing a chain is to pass the end link through a pin held in a vise, or a nail in the bench. With the chain held taut, pull a soft pad covered with rouge along the chain several times. Powdered rouge is best for chain polishing as there is less residue left behind.

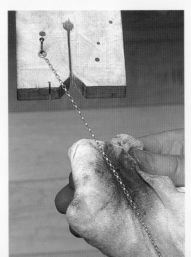

SAFETY CONSIDERATIONS

- Never polish a chain on a polishing machine without some support (see page 35) as the action of the mops could throw the chain out of your hand, causing serious injury.

PROJECT 1 OCTAGONAL RING

YOU WILL NEED

- 2⅛ in (54 mm) of ¹⁄₁₆ in (1.5 mm) thick wire
- Bench peg and vise
- Hand file
- Emery paper
- Parallel-jawed pliers
- Rolled-hide mallet
- Flat stake
- Soldering equipment (see page 31)
- Small piece of thin iron or copper wire
- Tapered mandrel
- Planishing hammer
- Polishing equipment (see page 34)

| TECHNIQUES COVERED ● Soldering ● Forming ● Planishing ● Polishing |

Many of the basic skills of jewelry making are employed in the making of this simple ring. Mastery of these skills makes possible the creation of a number of related projects. The length of wire suggested will accommodate all but the largest fingers as the forging process is used to stretch the ring to the required size. The keys to success in this project are to ensure that the two ends of the wire fit together perfectly with no gap between, and that the area around the join is clean and free from grease or oxide.

1 Push one end of the wire through a hole in the bench peg. File the surface of the bench peg while at the same time pushing the wire against the file to square off the end. Repeat with the other end of the wire so that both are completely flat.

2 Clean off the burr with emery paper folded over and held between the thumb and finger. Take care not to round off the sharp corners of the flat ends.

Emery paper will remove any oxide or grease from the surface of the metal.

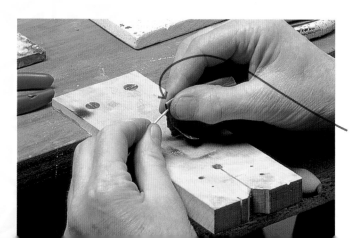

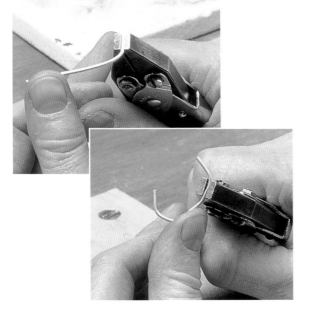

3 Bend the wire into shape in four stages with flat-jawed pliers using the width of the jaws as a guide, until both ends of the ring meet.

Do not tap so hard with the mallet that the ring becomes too flat to shape on the mandrel.

4 Gently tap down on the ring with a rolled-hide mallet until the two cut ends are perfectly aligned. The ends should now fit together perfectly.

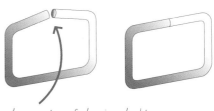

The top edges of the ring should slope upward as shown.

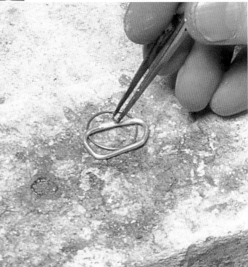

5 Paint the join with flux and place it on a firebrick (above). Use tweezers to place pallions of solder on the flux (right).

6 Heat the work gently at first to avoid boiling the flux. When the flux is dry, heat with more force, directing the flame toward the back of the ring at first, away from the join. Finally, concentrate the heat on the join, making sure that both sides get equally hot. As soon as the solder flows—not a moment longer—withdraw the heat.

7 Cool the ring in water and place it in the acid pickle—one part acid to five parts water—for five minutes to clean it (see page 33).

Lay a piece of thin iron or copper wire under the ring: this will raise it slightly off the surface and allow the free flow of molten solder around the join.

8 The ring is now ready to be shaped to fit. Place the ring on a tapered mandrel, and use a mallet to shape it. Tap the mallet against the ring, turning the mandrel as you do so until the ring is perfectly round.

slowly work the ring down the tapered mandrel as it becomes round.

9 To ensure that the ring is perfectly flat, place it on a flat stake and tap it with the mallet.

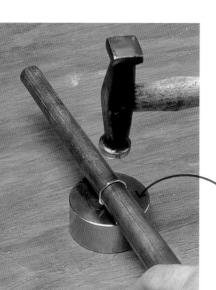

10 To finish the ring and give it its octagonal shape, it must be planished. With the ring on a tapered mandrel, hold it flat against the stake. Using a planishing hammer, form a flat surface on one side of the ring, creating one side of the octagon, then turn it around to reinforce the opposite side. Repeat this on all eight sides then polish.

Ensure that your work surface is solid and sturdy.

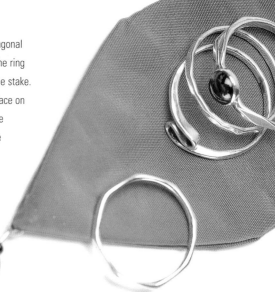

PROJECT 2 S-SHAPED RING

YOU WILL NEED
- Round silver wire
  2¾ x ¹⁄₁₆ in
  (70 x 1.5 mm)
- Soldering
  equipment (see
  page 31)
- Tapered mandrel
- Rolled-hide mallet
- Flat stake
- Round-nosed pliers
- Parallel-jawed
  pliers
- Hand file
- Planishing hammer
- Polishing
  equipment (see
  page 34)

| TECHNIQUES COVERED ● Soldering ● Annealing ● Polishing |

The making of this ring develops further the techniques used on the octagonal ring (see page 38). The twisted design allows for some adjustment to the ring size.

1 Begin by soldering the wire into a ring. Make the ring round using the mandrel and mallet, then flatten it by placing it on the stake and tapping it with the mallet. Hammer a series of flats to give the ring its octagonal shape (see Steps 8–10, page 40), but this time leave three out of the eight sections untouched. With the ring held flat on the stake, hammer down the corners between the flats on the untouched section.

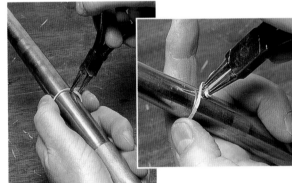

Flatten the ring on five out of eight sections.

2 Hammer the remaining round wire so that there is a smooth transition from flat on the back to a vertical flat on the front. Anneal and then polish, paying particular attention to the vertical front section as this will be difficult to polish at the end.

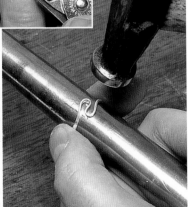

Hammer the round front section flat.

3 Place the ring loosely on the mandrel and with round-nosed pliers twist the front section into an "S" shape; as you do so, try the ring for size. Do not grip the wire with the pliers but keep the jaws apart with your finger as you twist.

4 Straighten the back (or shank) of the ring by squeezing with parallel pliers held just behind the "S" shape. Planish the ring lightly all round on the mandrel to restore its roundness and remove any remaining corners and bumps, then give it a final polish.

PROJECT 3 PLANISHED BANGLE

YOU WILL NEED

- Strip of bronze
  6¾ x ½ x ½ in
  (170 x 12 x 1 mm)
- 19⁄32 in (15 mm)
  diameter coin
- Scriber
- Jeweler's shears
- Hand file
- Emery boards of
  various grades
- Domed stake
- Planishing hammer
- Annealing
  equipment (see
  page 30)
- Polishing equipment
  (see page 34)
- Rolled hide mallet
- 1³⁷⁄₆₄/1³¹⁄₃₂ in (40/50mm)
  diameter round
  former, metal or
  wood

TECHNIQUES COVERED ● Cutting ● Planishing ● Annealing ● Forming ● Polishing

This bronze bangle is planished using both ends of a ball-peen hammer, the edge being finished with the flat face of the hammer after the center section has been planished with the ball peen. If you work right up to an edge with a ball peen the work can become distorted, but the flat face of the hammer is more easily controlled and gives the edge a more finished look.

1 Using a coin about 19⁄32 in (15 mm) in diameter as a guide, scribe an arc on each end of the bronze strip.

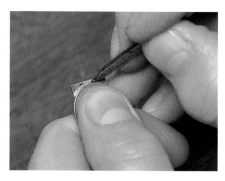

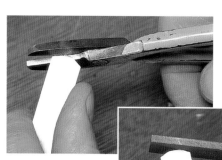

2 Trim the ends with jeweler's shears, then finish with a file and emery boards.

You should aim to sandwich the metal between hammer and stake with no gaps between.

3 Place the strip on a slightly domed stake and planish it with the ball-peen hammer. Try to bring the hammer down on the same spot on the stake, moving the strip beneath it. The aim is to sandwich the work between hammer and stake with no gap. Listen for the hollow sound of the hammer missing the point of contact.

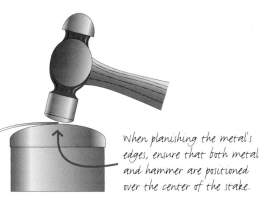

4 Avoid the edge of the metal as a ball peen-hammer will distort it. When all the surface is evenly covered with hammer marks, work on the edges with the flat side of the hammer. Position the edge of the metal over the center of the stake and use just half of the hammer.

When planishing the metal's edges, ensure that both metal and hammer are positioned over the center of the stake.

5 Now anneal the work and polish it, holding it against a piece of wood.

6 First place one end on a round former. Then bend it by striking it with a mallet just beyond the point of contact with the former. Repeat with the other end. Once the ends are formed, it is easy to bend the middle section to shape using your fingers.

PROJECT 4 FORGED CHOKER AND EARRINGS

YOU WILL NEED

- End cutters
- 11¹³⁄₁₆ x ⁵⁄₆₄ in (300 x 2 mm) round silver wire
- Planishing hammer and domed stake
- Parallel-jawed pliers
- Center punch
- Steel plate
- Electric drill and ¹⁄₁₆ in (1.5 mm) bit
- Wood block
- 19¾ x ⁵⁄₆₄ in (500 x 1.3 mm) round silver wire
- Hand file
- Round-nosed pliers
- Round former, such as mug or paint can
- Polishing equipment (see page 34)
- Six ¹⁵⁄₆₄ in (6 mm) round beads
- 2 x ¹⁄₃₂ in (50 x 1 mm) wire
- Pair of earring hook wires

Forging describes the process of shaping metal with hammers in order to change the form of the metal significantly. This is as opposed to planishing where only the surface of the metal is treated.

1 First make the seven units that hang from the choker and the two earrings. Use end cutters to cut the 11¹³⁄₁₆ x ⁵⁄₆₄ in (300 x 2 mm) silver wire into nine pieces of the following lengths: one of 1³⁷⁄₆₄ in (40 mm), four of 1⅜ in (35 mm), two of 1³⁄₁₆ in (30 mm), and two of 1 in (25 mm). Begin forging by hammering the end of the wire at an angle.

2 Now work along the wire until you have achieved a gradual taper from round to flat.

3 Turn the unit by 90 degrees and repeat the hammering process at the other end of the wire, this time holding the thin metal with parallel-jawed pliers to keep it square to the hammer.

4 Having trimmed the ends with end cutters, mark out the hole at one end of each unit and center punch. Seven of the units will hang from the choker, the remaining two will be used for the earrings.

5 Then, using the drill, drill a hole through the end of each unit. Holding the wire with a finger while drilling is quite safe. If the drill should jam, a nail will prevent the work from spinning around with the drill.

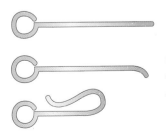

The earrings are made using two units that match those of the choker. Connect two 1⅜ × ¹/₁₆ in (35 × 2 mm) forged pieces to the earring hook wires with jump rings of ¹/₂₅ in (1 mm) wire.

6 Using the end cutters, cut the 19¾ × ³/₆₄ in (500 × 1.3 mm) round silver wire into two pieces, 15 in (380 mm) and 4¾ in (120 mm) long. The longer piece will be the choker necklace. Prepare to make an eye at either end of the necklace by filing each end flat then bending it sharply about ¹⁹/₃₂ in (15 mm) from the end as shown. Now with round-nosed pliers you will be able to create an eye square to the wire.

7 Bend the choker around a round former. Planish it lightly to make it springy then use a cloth to polish it—a thin wire object of this kind is difficult to polish safely on the polishing machine. Use the remaining 4¾ in (120 mm) of wire to make a small chain to connect the two ends of the choker necklace. This is assembled from jump rings of ¼ in (6 mm) and ⁵/₃₂ in (4 mm) in diameter (see page 120). If all the rings are work hardened by repeatedly bending them back and forth, there should be no need to solder them closed.

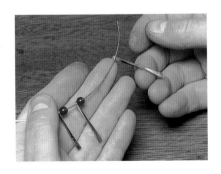

8 After polishing the units, thread the shortest onto the necklace first, followed by a bead. Then thread the next longest unit, followed by a bead, and so on. The finished ensemble should feature the longest unit at the center with progressively shorter units to either side. Remember that two of the second longest pieces are going on the earrings. Make an eye on each end of the choker wire and attach the jump rings to one of them.

9 Make a hook from 2 × ³/₆₄ in (50 × 1.3 mm) of wire. Begin by forming an eye as you did on the end of the choker wire. Round off one end and polish it. Using the widest end of the round-nosed pliers, bend the other end, then bend the hook in the opposite direction so that the end comes just short of the eye. Planish the bend to harden it. Attach the hook to the other eye at the end of the choker necklace.

Create the choker's closing hook in three stages as shown left.

YOU WILL NEED
- End cutters
- 4 x ⁵⁄₆₄ in (100 x 2 mm) silver wire
- Flat stake
- Planishing hammer
- Flat punch
- Soldering equipment (see page 31) including a charcoal block
- Phillips head screw countersunk into a steel bar
- Domed stake
- Annealing equipment (see page 30)
- Electric drill and ¹⁄₁₆ in (1.5 mm) drill
- Wood block
- Small weight
- Polishing equipment (see page 34)
- Two ear posts and butterflies

PROJECT 5 SILVER CROSS AND EAR STUDS

TECHNIQUES COVERED ● Cutting ● Soldering ● Annealing ● Drilling ● Polishing

In this project, forging is taken a step further. The arms on the cross are forged in the same way as the elements of the choker in the previous project (page 44). The join of the cross is created by forging and the little boss in the center is an example of forging using a mold or pattern.

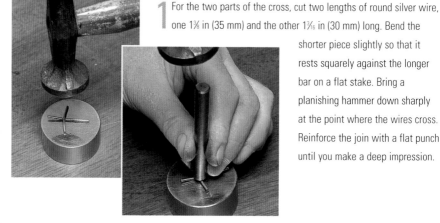

1 For the two parts of the cross, cut two lengths of round silver wire, one 1⅜ in (35 mm) and the other 1³⁄₁₆ in (30 mm) long. Bend the shorter piece slightly so that it rests squarely against the longer bar on a flat stake. Bring a planishing hammer down sharply at the point where the wires cross. Reinforce the join with a flat punch until you make a deep impression.

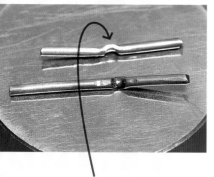

At this stage you can file off the little swelling either side of the join.

2 As you force one wire into the other the surplus metal bulges out at the sides. This metal will be hidden by the silver boss, but if you decide not to include the boss, the swelling should be removed with a file before soldering.

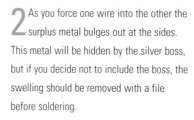

3 Solder the two parts together, ensuring that two pallions of easy solder are touching both pieces of wire.

4 Now forge the four arms of the cross on the domed stake in the same way as for each element of the choker (see Steps 1–3, page 44).

5 Cut the remainder of the silver wire into three equal parts, each ¹⁵⁄₃₂ in (12 mm) long to make the bosses and two ear studs. Heat each part, one in turn, with flux until it melts into a bead, then place this on top of a Phillips head screw head set in a steel bar. Use the flat punch to forge the bead into the form of a tiny cross.

6 Forging the metal causes work hardening. So after the first few blows, anneal the silver with a gentle flame. If the silver gets stuck in the screw head, use the end cutters to pull it out, place the silver on the screw head and continue forging until the silver covers the screw head.

7 Use the end cutters to trim the finished forging on each of the three elements to an even square or octagon.

8 Very careful positioning is required when soldering the boss into place. Make a small indent with a drill in the charcoal block, then place the boss face down, having first coated it with solder. Now place the cleaned and fluxed cross in position with a small weight to prevent it twisting when the solder remelts.

9 Trim the ends of the cross with end cutters, taking particular care to leave both sides of the horizontal bar the same length.

10 After drilling and polishing, fit a jump ring (see page 120) to allow hanging from a chain. Soldering the ear studs requires two stages. Melt solder onto the back of each forging, then rest the work in the same charcoal block to reheat, with the fluxed ear post balancing on top.

PROJECT 6 DOMED EAR STUDS

YOU WILL NEED

- ⅞ x ½₂ in (22 x 1 mm) strip of silver
- Permanent marker pen
- Punch and die
- Heavy hammer
- Vise
- Annealing equipment (see page 30)
- Doming block and doming punches
- Emery paper
- Ball-peen hammer
- Pair of ear posts and butterflies
- Wooden punch with a ½₂ in (1 mm) hole
- Soldering equipment (see page 31)

TECHNIQUES COVERED ● Annealing ● Soldering

Precise domes are easily made with a doming block. Wooden punches are simple to make from dowel wood; they are less likely to damage the pattern on your work, and, unlike steel punches, will never leave marks on the brass doming block. The punch and die consists simply of two pieces of steel bolted together, with holes drilled and punches made to fit. Punches are made from mild steel with the face ground off at a slight angle. The other end is ground to a chamfer to prevent mushrooming. Use shears or a piercing saw if you do not have a punch and die.

The strip of metal is sandwiched between the two faces of the die and the three screws tightened securely before hammering.

1 Begin by drawing two lines on the back of the silver strip, equidistant from each side. This will help you line it up in the die. Place the silver face down in one face of the die, place the other face on top, and tighten the screws securely. Position the die over a bench leg. Strike several blows with a heavy hammer to punch out a disc. Repeat to punch out a second disc.

2 Anneal the discs, then place them face down in the smallest hollow of a doming block that will accommodate them without overlapping the edge. Use a hammer and a wooden punch to create a shallow dome. As the dome takes shape it will fit the next smallest hollow. Move the disc to the next hollow and punch again. Continue until the desired dome shape is reached.

3 Rub the edges down on a flat surface covered with emery paper, then planish the edges using a ball-peen hammer held in the vise as a stake.

4 The plate on the end of the ear post is flat and must be domed to fit before it is soldered to the dome. This will ensure that there are no gaps between the two surfaces to be soldered. Use a round wooden punch with a hole in the end to hold the ear post in the smallest hollow that formed the dome. Hammer the post into the mold so that it takes the same shape as the dome. Repeat with the second post.

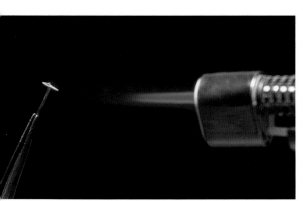

5 Soldering the ear post to the back of the dome is best carried out in two stages. First melt easy solder onto the post plate.

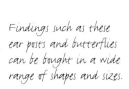

Findings such as these ear posts and butterflies can be bought in a wide range of shapes and sizes.

6 Then, having cleaned and fluxed the inside of the dome, heat the whole piece. Hold the post in tweezers locked on with a little ring and balanced to allow the post to settle into position when the solder re-melts. The flame must be directed to the bottom of the dome where it touches the firebrick. Repeat to complete the second earring.

CHAPTER 2

FURTHER TECHNIQUES and PROJECTS

Now that you have learned the basic skills of jewelry making, you can move on to more advanced and sophisticated techniques and projects. Although it is not possible to demonstrate all the techniques of jewelry making in a single book, the techniques shown here lay the foundation for what is a hugely rewarding and multi-faceted craft.

This chapter covers several important areas of jewelry making, including wire work, etching, melting and fusing, repoussé, and stone setting. The lessons at the beginning of each section present the core techniques, while the ensuing projects use and expand on the lessons, by employing them in the context of creating a specific item of jewelry.

You can adapt most of the projects in this section to suit your own tastes and needs, but however you use them there will be plenty to interest and inspire you.

WORKING IN WIRE

Wire in its infinitely varied forms has been used for centuries by every kind of metal worker. Dies made of agate are thought to have been used for making wire in 2500 B.C. Armorers have used wire for the embellishment of sword handles, silversmiths have used it for the decoration of bowls and chalices, and the jewelry maker has found in wire a medium as versatile as his imagination. Wire can be drawn into different sections and sizes and it can be bent, twisted, rolled, drawn, forged, or planished. It can also be used to make chains. The scroll form alone offers a bewildering range of possibilities, and fine wire is even used for knitting and crochet work. This section uses copper and silver wire to demonstrate the many techniques of working in wire. All wire is made by drawing metal through successively smaller holes in drawplates or dies. The property that metals possess that makes this process possible is called ductility. All metals are ductile with the notable exception of lead. Gold is the most ductile of all metals—from just one ounce (28 g) of pure gold enough wire can be produced to stretch for fifty miles (80 km).

As an introduction to jewelry making, wire work is ideal, since wire is the most accessible form of metal available to us. In its annealed state, non-ferrous metal wire can be worked with accuracy, using little force. Anyone can bend a piece of wire and, apart from the drawplate and the bending jig, you require only basic tools to make the projects in this section.

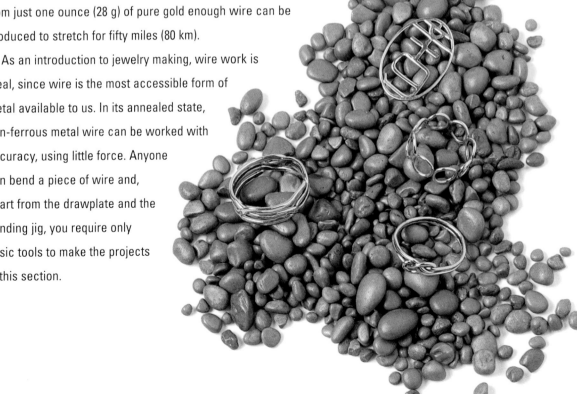

LESSON: WIRE DRAWING

Drawing wire involves pulling it through a drawplate which has consecutively smaller holes. As the wire is pulled through smaller and smaller holes, it becomes longer and thinner. The holes in a drawplate range from $\frac{5}{32}$ or $\frac{13}{64}$ in (4 or 5 mm) down to as fine as the eye can see. Shapes available include round, half round, oval, square, fluted, and bearer wire.

YOU WILL NEED

- Bench peg and vise
- Vise guards or cloth
- Drawplate for drawing wire
- Soldering torch
- Wire
- Hand file
- Annealing equipment (see page 30)
- Engineer's pliers
- Strip of sheet metal
- Steel rod
- Swage block
- Wood block
- Hammer
- Rolled-hide mallet
- Drawplate
- Engineer's pliers

DRAWPLATES

A great many drawplates with various shapes and sizes are available commercially. When you buy a wire drawplate, make sure there isn't much difference in size between one hole and the next—the wire must be pulled through with such force that significant gradations of hole size can cause the wire to break. It is also a good idea to lubricate the drawplate with beeswax occasionally. Do this by warming the drawplate with a blowtorch, then rubbing the back with the beeswax.

Lubricating drawplates with beeswax allows the wire to be drawn through the holes easily.

MEDIUM TO THICK WIRE

1 The wire to be drawn must have a gradual taper, called a leader, filed on its end. This should be about $\frac{19}{32}$ to $\frac{25}{32}$ in (15 to 20 mm) long, tapering to about half its diameter at the end. A leader must not be thin to a point—if the end is too fine it may break off. The leader allows for enough wire protruding beyond the hole to be gripped by the pliers. Always make more than your immediate requirements; it is as easy to draw down 40 or 80 in (1 or 2 m) as 20 in (0.5 m).

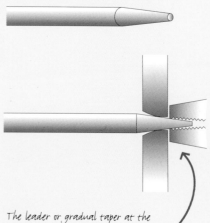

The leader or gradual taper at the end of the wire allows enough wire to protrude through the hole to be gripped by the pliers.

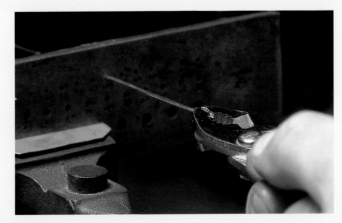

2 If working with thin wire (less than ⅟₁₆ in [1.5 mm] in diameter), all you need are a drawplate held in a vise and a pair of engineer's pliers. Protect the vise with vise guards or cloth so that the drawplate does not get marked in the vise, and fasten the drawplate into the vise.

3 The front of the drawplate has numbers that correspond to the diameter of the holes and the thickness of the wire they will produce. On the back of the drawplate the holes appear bigger. Choose a hole one size smaller than the wire diameter. Thread the wire through a hole from the back. The taper should come out the other side but the wire should be too thick to pass through. Use engineer's pliers to pull the wire through the hole. Repeat the process, passing the wire through a succession of smaller and smaller holes until it reaches the size you want it to be.

Drawplates.

4 Regular annealing is needed to prevent breakage of the wire due to work hardening. Take care to soften the entire length as any small section left hard will lead to a breakage. If in doubt go over the wire again; annealing parts of the wire more than once will do no harm.

MAKING RECTANGULAR WIRE
You can create wire with a rectangular cross-section by soldering a double length of wire and drawing it through a drawplate with square-shaped holes.

CHENIER

1 Fine tubing called "chenier" is made from a flat strip tapered at one end. This is hammered into a "U" section around a steel rod in a swage block. Place the swage block on a wood block.

Strip is tapered at one end.

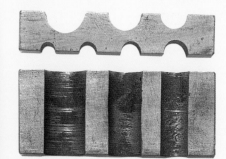

Metal swage block
viewed from side
and above..

2 Tap it into shape with a mallet then draw it through several holes in the drawplate.

3 After drawing down, secure the almost invisible seam by soldering. When a length of wire is drawn within a chenier, the inside diameter is preserved; the perfect fit between the chenier and the internal wire is useful for making hinges and other findings.

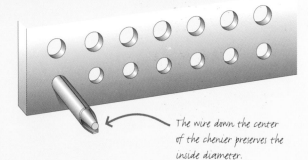

The wire down the center
of the chenier preserves the
inside diameter.

Examples of drawn wire and chenier.

Chenier can
be used for
findings
such as this.

PROJECT 7 BASIC SCROLL RING

YOU WILL NEED
- Hand file
- Bench peg
- 4¾ x 3⁄64 in (120 x 1.3 mm) round silver wire
- Round-nosed pliers
- Annealing equipment (see page 30)
- Jump ring
- Parallel-jawed pliers
- Paper
- Soldering equipment (see page 31)
- Rolled-hide mallet
- Tapered mandrel
- Planishing hammer
- Polishing equipment (see page 34)

TECHNIQUES COVERED ● Annealing ● Planishing ● Soldering ● Forging ● Polishing

You can use scroll forms to create all kinds of jewelry. The numerous possibilities offered by scrollwork make it worthwhile practicing with pliers and scraps of copper wire until you can create a smooth scroll without kinks or straight sections. As you practice you will build up a collection of scrolls that will be a useful designing aid. Note the length of wire you start with while it is still straight. You may need to know how long it was later—and measuring it after you have bent it into a scroll is nearly impossible. This silver ring makes a good introduction to scroll jewelry. The ring's two scrolls are identical in pattern, but they need not be.

1 Begin by filing the end of the silver wire into a gradual taper on a bench peg. Any scroll is improved by this refinement and the thinner section will make the first part of the scroll much easier to form. The taper need only be on one side of the wire. In this way the finished scroll will be the same thickness right into its center. You may find it easier to hold the wire with pliers as you file it.

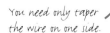

You need only taper the wire on one side.

2 Push a thin wire jump ring on one jaw of a pair of round-nosed pliers. Anneal the wire, then hold one end against the jump ring on the pliers, to help you make the scrolls identical. Take care not to damage the wire by squeezing too hard. As you bend the wire around one jaw, allow the other jaw to slide off the end of the wire—this will ensure a fully rounded end to your scroll.

As the scroll gets bigger it will be possible to roll it up with finger and thumb.

3 When you have created a small semicircle, you can grip the wire more firmly using parallel-jawed pliers. Continue by either pulling, bending, or squeezing, moving the wire around in the jaws as you proceed. Then make a similar scroll in the opposite direction at the other end of the wire.

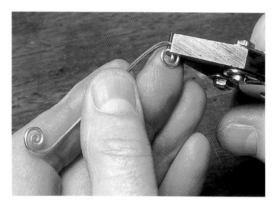

4 At this point you must consider the final size of the ring. The distance between the two points of contact is the circumference, but planishing will make the ring larger. Take a strip of paper, wrap it around the finger and mark the finger size. Then subtract ¹³⁄₆₄ in (5 mm) to give the ring size. Bend the two ends up with pliers. Using your fingers, shape the wire into a ring until the two scrolls are firmly pressed together.

5 Solder the scrolls together using easy solder. Rest the scrolls on wires and direct the flame along the join. Keep the flame clear of the scroll ends, which tend to be vulnerable to overheating.

6 After making the ring round using a rolled-hide mallet on a tapered mandrel, use parallel-jawed pliers to remove any kinks, before planishing and, finally, polishing.

YOU WILL NEED

- Bench peg
- 4, 3, and 2½ in (102, 75, and 68 mm) lengths of ¾₄ in (1.3 mm) round silver wire
- Hand file
- Jump ring
- Round-nosed pliers
- Permanent marker pen
- Parallel-jawed pliers
- Soldering equipment (see page 31)
- Planishing hammer and domed stake
- Polishing equipment (see page 34)
- 3, 2 and 1¾ in (75, 55 and 45 mm) lengths of ¾₄ in (1.1 mm) silver wire

PROJECT 8 SCROLL PENDANT WITH EARRINGS

TECHNIQUES COVERED ● Annealing ● Soldering ● Planishing ● Polishing

This scroll pendant with matching earrings opens up the many possibilities presented by scrolls used in combination. By varying the lengths of wire used and making slight alterations to the shape and position of each element, you can make a big difference to the appearance of the finished pendant.

1 Form the three lengths of ¾₄ in (1.3 mm) wire into scrolls (see Steps 1–3, pages 56–57), bending the curves with your fingers and trying each element against its neighbor until you are satisfied with the arrangement.

2 It is easier to solder the four joins if you flatten the points of contact for a better fit. Lay the three components in position and mark the points of contact with a permanent pen.

3 Holding the work with the parallel-jawed pliers, file a slight flat against each mark.

When soldering, work on the far side so that the flame does not harm the rest of the work

4 Solder from the reverse as the underside of this kind of join invariably turns out best. Take care to direct the flame along the join away from the scroll ends.

5 When planishing, try to direct the hammer toward some sections more than others. This will vary the width of the wire when viewed from the front. Polish. Use the three lengths of the ¾₄ in (1.1 mm) wire to make scroll earrings in the same way.

YOU WILL NEED
- Bench peg
- Hand file
- Four 6 x ¹⁄₁₆ in (150 x 1.5 mm) lengths of round silver wire
- Annealing equipment (see page 30)
- Parallel-jawed pliers
- Jump ring
- Round-nosed pliers
- Piece of wood or metal with hole drilled in it
- Soldering equipment (see page 31)
- A hollow vessel
- Planishing hammer and domed stake
- Polishing equipment (see page 34)
- 8 x ¹⁄₁₆ in (200 x 1.5 mm) round silver wire

PROJECT 9 SCROLL VARIATION: HAIR ORNAMENT

TECHNIQUES COVERED ● Annealing ● Soldering ● Planishing ● Polishing

This silver hair ornament has closed scrolls, which provide accommodation for the pin. Make a model in copper first to give you some practice and the opportunity to try out different arrangements and designs.

1 For this kind of scroll, file the ends of the four 6 in (150 mm) wires almost to a point. This will allow the end to fit neatly against the wire to create the scroll. After annealing, form the first part of the scroll (see Steps 1–3, pages 56–57), then bend the wire into a complete ring using the round-nosed pliers. Make this ring a little smaller than you want the finished ring to be.

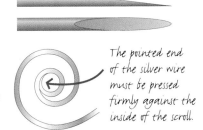

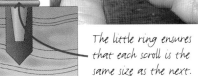

The pointed end of the silver wire must be pressed firmly against the inside of the scroll.

2 As the scroll begins to take shape, push the jaw of the round-nosed pliers into the center of the scroll to force the end against the wire. Support the work on a piece of wood or metal with a hole drilled to allow the point of the jaw to pass through. Using a jump ring on the jaw will ensure that the holes are all the same size. Note that the two holes at the center of this ornament are slightly smaller than the others.

The little ring ensures that each scroll is the same size as the next.

3 When the scrolls are complete, solder each little ring closed. Assemble the hair ornament in stages—solder the top and bottom scrolls together first before adding each side piece.

4 When all the parts are joined, press the piece into a hollow vessel with your fingers—a ladle or small bowl will do. Planish the piece on a domed stake. Finally, polish the piece, ideally with polishing pads.

5 Use 8 x ¹⁄₁₆ in (200 x 1.5 mm) round silver wire to make the scroll on the end of the pin in the same way as you made the other scrolls. Make the pin about 4¾ in (120 mm) long, creating kinks with parallel-jawed pliers about halfway down. Round off the point.

PROJECT 10 CELTIC SCROLL PENDANT

YOU WILL NEED

- 6¾ x ½ in (170 x 1 mm) round silver wire
- End cutters
- Flat stake
- Hammer
- Flat punch
- Soldering equipment (see page 31)
- Ruler
- Bench peg
- Smooth hand file
- Annealing equipment (see page 30)
- Round-nosed pliers
- Parallel-jawed pliers
- 3³⁄₁₆ x ³⁄₆₄ in (80 x 1.2 mm) round silver wire
- Tapered mandrel
- Rolled-hide mallet
- Planishing hammer
- Polishing equipment (see page 34)
- Leather thong

| TECHNIQUES COVERED ● Cutting ● Annealing ● Soldering ● Forming ● Planishing ● Polishing |

This simple scroll pendant is made by shaping and planishing silver wire and can be created in a variety of shapes and sizes. Try sketching out a few alternative designs on a page beforehand and then choose your favorite to create in silver.

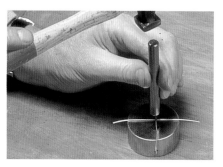

Aim the heat away from the join at first.

1 Cut two 3¹³⁄₃₂ in (85 mm) lengths of ½ in (1 mm) round silver wire. Place them on a flat stake in a cross shape and then punch them into position with a hammer and a flat punch.

2 Solder the two wires together, placing the cross on a small ring of iron or copper wire to lift it slightly off the firebrick. This will ensure that both pieces of metal will heat evenly.

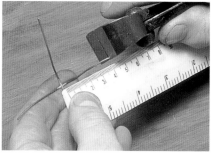

3 Measure each side of the cross and trim each length to exactly 1³⁷⁄₆₄ in (40 mm). This ensures that each scroll will be the same size.

4 To taper the ends, make a groove in the bench peg and rest one of the ends of the cross in it. File the end flat with a smooth hand file (see page 56).

Hold the piece in the center of the cross to ensure a firm grip while forming the scrolls.

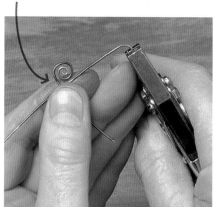

5 Anneal the piece, then use a pair of round-nosed pliers to scroll the wire. Start with the very end of the wire and wrap it around letting the pliers slide off the end. Then use a pair of parallel-jawed pliers to pull and bend the wire toward the center of the cross forming a smooth, even scroll.

To work out the length of wire needed for the circle surround, multiply the width of the scroll shape by 3.14

6 Use your fingers to push the last twist of the scroll in place. Repeat on all four sections of the cross.

7 To make the ring surround, first measure the scroll shape indent. It should be about 1 in (25 mm) across. For this size of scroll you will need about 3³⁄₁₆ in (80 mm) of ³⁄₆₄ in (1.2 mm) silver wire for the surround. With the techniques used to make the octagonal ring (see Steps 1–6, pages 38–40), bend the wire until the squared-off ends meet, and then solder. Use a hard solder as the join will be heated twice and may spring apart on second heating. Once soldered, place in acid pickle for about five minutes.

Ensure that the pallions touch both the wire on the scroll and on the circle.

8 Work the ring into a round shape using a tapered mandrel and mallet, then flatten using a mallet on the flat stake. Place the scroll shape inside the ring and check the fit. If the ring surround is too small, you can stretch it on the mandrel using a planishing hammer. Tweak the scrolls slightly until they fit perfectly inside the circle. Mix the flux and paint it on the four "corners" of the scroll where it touches the circle. Using tweezers, pick up pallions of solder and place them carefully on the four joins.

9 Heat each join with the soldering torch until the solder melts and flows. Direct the heat toward the ring at first and away from the joins, as the thicker wire of the ring will take longer to reach the required temperature.

10 Drop the pendant in the acid solution to clean for about five minutes. Remove and flatten the pendant using a planishing hammer. Planishing may distort the scrolls slightly, but this is easily corrected using the tips of the round-nosed pliers. To finish, polish and tie with a leather thong.

LESSON: TWISTED WIRE

Twisted wire patterns have many applications. They can be used to embellish the settings for stones and for making bangles, rings, necklaces, and parts of chains. Different sections of wire, various combinations of metal and of gauges can be used to create all kinds of designs. Experimenting with copper wire is recommended. Always anneal your wire before and during twisting.

YOU WILL NEED

- Round copper wire, at least 8 x ¹⁄₁₆ in (200 x 1.5 mm)
- Annealing equipment (see page 30)
- Vise
- Steel rod
- Soldering equipment (see page 31)
- Planishing hammer and flat stake
- Rolling mill
- Drawplate

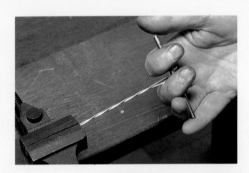

1 Take a length of round wire, at least 8 x ¹⁄₁₆ in (200 x 1.5 mm), bend it double, then anneal it. Tighten the loose ends in a vise and, with a steel rod through the other end, twist the double wire, pulling slightly as you do so.

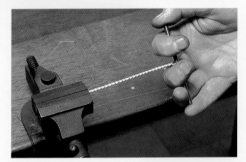

2 After about twenty turns the two wires take on the appearance of a rope.

3 Now solder the two wires together. Flux well, then wipe off most of the flux so that it only remains in the hollows. Use small pallions, one in every other twist. As the flame passes down the work, the solder will melt between the wires.

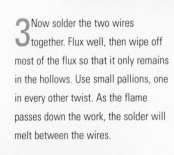

4 You may now hammer the twisted wire, pass it through a rolling mill, or through a drawplate to create different effects. For a variety of effects you can try: not soldering the two wires together; twisting metals of different colors or shapes; twisting more tightly or less; or using square wire or flat wire twisted by itself.

PROJECT 11 TWISTED RING

YOU WILL NEED
- 4 x ¹⁄₁₆ in (100 x 1.5 mm) round silver wire
- 4 x ¹⁄₁₆ in (100 x 1.5 mm) round copper wire
- Soldering equipment (see page 31)
- Annealing equipment (see page 30)
- Vise
- ¹³⁄₆₄ in (5 mm) steel rod
- Piercing saw
- Hand file
- Parallel-jawed pliers
- Bench peg
- Planishing hammer
- Tapered mandrel
- Polishing equipment (see page 34)

TECHNIQUES COVERED ● Soldering ● Planishing ● Annealing ● Twisting Wire ● Cutting ● Forming

In making this twisted ring of silver and copper the two wires undergo a complete transformation. You may prefer to use one of the twisted forms discussed on page 62 as an alternative design.

Butt join.

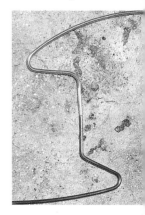

1 Begin by soldering the ends of the two wires together. A butt join will be strong enough to withstand the twisting process. Bend both wires to help keep them in place during soldering.

There must be a number of complete twists for the two ends of the ring to match.

2 Anneal the joined wire, bend it double, and fasten the loose ends in a vise. Using the steel rod, twist the two wires together for about ten turns. Now decide how long you want your ring to be; this design will expand by about ²⁵⁄₆₄ in (10 mm). You may need to twist a little more. Solder the twisted wires together, then cut to the required length with a piercing saw.

3 You may now file each end of the ring flat using the hole in the bench peg. Bend the twisted wires into a ring with parallel-jawed pliers. If you have calculated correctly the two ends should fit together—silver to silver and copper to copper.

4 Solder the join. Use slightly more solder than you would ordinarily use as some of the solder will leak out into the join between the wires. Clean off any excess solder from around the join with a file, then planish on a tapered mandrel until the ring is a perfect fit. Polish.

YOU WILL NEED
- 14 x 1/16 in (360 x 1.5 mm) gilding metal wire
- Hand file
- Bench peg
- Binding wire
- Soldering equipment (see page 31)
- Two steel rods
- Vise
- Annealing equipment (see page 30)
- Tapered mandrel
- Block of wood or metal with a series of holes
- Planishing hammer and flat stake
- Scraps of silver
- Polishing equipment (see page 34)
- Round former

PROJECT 12 TWISTED WIRE BANGLE

TECHNIQUES COVERED • Soldering • Annealing • Twisting Wire • Polishing • Forming

This gilding metal bangle provides a solution to the problem of what to do with the crushed ends of wire that have been gripped in the vise during twisting. In this project, the loose ends are eliminated by joining them in a long loop to be twisted between two steel rods. The necessary force can therefore be applied without damage to the round wire.

1 File both ends of the gilding metal wire flat using the hole in the bench peg. Form the wire into a double loop and bind with wire temporarily. This will make it easier to line up the ends for soldering. Use hard solder to join up the ends of the wire.

2 Open the wire so that it forms a continuous loop. Hold one steel rod in a vise and place a loop over the rod. Pull the loop with the other rod and begin twisting. Arrange for the join to be at one end.

3 Anneal and continue twisting until the metal has a rope-like appearance. If one end begins to twist more tightly than the other, stop and twist from the other end. Solder the twists together at the ends, leaving a loop at either end.

4 Open out the loops and make them round by placing them over a hole in a wood or metal block and tappping in a tapered mandrel.

5 Planish each end until the area around the holes is an even thickness. Now ball up some scraps of silver until you have two beads that fit your loops perfectly (see page 47). This process may take several attempts. Solder each bead into place from the back, using four pallions of easy solder. Polish, using a strip of wood as a support, then bend to shape around a former such as a rolling pin.

PROJECT 13 HORSESHOE BANGLE

TECHNIQUES COVERED ● Annealing ● Twisting Wire ● Planishing ● Drilling ● Polishing

An alternative method of tidying up loose ends of wire is shown in the making of this bangle with a horseshoe catch made in silver. The length of wire suggested will make a bangle to fit the average wrist.

YOU WILL NEED

- 16 x ¹⁄₁₆ in (400 x 1.5 mm) round silver wire
- Annealing equipment (see page 30)
- Vise
- Small screwdriver
- ⁵⁄₃₂ in (4 mm) steel rod
- End cutters
- Hand file
- Planishing hammer and flat stake
- Round-nosed pliers
- 2 x ⁵⁄₆₄ in (50 x 2 mm) round silver wire
- Electric drill and ¹⁄₁₆ in (1.5 mm) bit
- Nail
- Soldering equipment (see page 31)
- Wooden block
- Polishing equipment (see page 34)
- Round fomer

1 Double the annealed silver wire and grip the loose ends in a vise. Insert a screwdriver in the loop against the vise and using a ⁵⁄₃₂ in (4 mm) steel rod, twist until you are happy with the look of your wire; there are about 50 twists in this version. The screwdriver leaves a short length of undamaged, untwisted wire.

2 From the looped end that was held in the screwdriver, trim the wire to leave two ends of about ²⁵⁄₆₄ in (10 mm) long each of free wire. Straighten and file a little taper on each end.

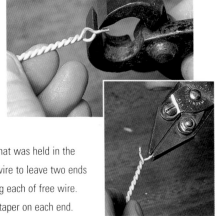

3 Hammer the ⁵⁄₆₄ in (2 mm) silver wire until it is about ⅛ in (3 mm) wide for 1³⁄₁₆ in (30 mm) of its length. Drill two ¹⁄₁₆ in (1.5 mm) holes ⅛ in (2.5 mm) apart near the end of this flat strip. Use a nail to prevent the wire spinning round with the drill. Remove the burrs from the holes.

4 Thread the tapered ends of the twisted wire through the holes in the flattened silver wire and trim the strip to 1³⁄₁₆ in (30 mm). Solder it into place on the twisted wire using pallions of easy solder placed against protruding wires.

5 Use end cutters to trim off the protruding ends of the twisted wire. Then file them with a hand file and emery boards, and polish. Now bend the bar down at the end, then over to form a little horseshoe shape. After polishing, using a wooden block as a support, bend the bangle around a former. The hook is held in the looped end of the twisted wire.

YOU WILL NEED
- 4¾ in x ⅙ (120 x 2 mm) round silver wire
- Vise
- Annealing equipment (see page 30)
- Steel rod
- Soldering equipment (see page 31)
- 8 x ¹⁄₃₂ in (200 x 1 mm) round gilding metal wire
- Serrated-jawed pliers
- Piercing saw
- Planishing hammer and domed stake
- Parallel-jawed pliers
- Hand file
- Emery boards
- End cutters
- Center punch
- Steel plate
- Electric drill with ⅙ in (1.5 mm) bit
- Polishing equipment (see pgae 34)

PROJECT 14 TWISTED AND FORGED PENDANT

TECHNIQUES COVERED ● Annealing ● Twisting Wire ● Soldering ● Cutting ● Planishing ● Polishing

This little pendant consists of heavy silver wire with thin gilding metal wire added to it. As the gilding metal becomes tarnished the contrast between the two metals is enhanced. The process of forging is used to transform the twisted round form into a triangular solid.

1 Double the silver wire and grip the loose ends in the vise. Anneal the silver wire then, with a steel rod through the other end, twist for about seven or eight turns. Solder the twists together, using one large pallion for every twist. There must be a surplus of solder in the join. Anneal the gilding metal wire. Then, with the silver still in the vise, thread the gilding metal through the loop held in the vise and double it. Hold both ends of the gilding metal firmly with serrated-jawed pliers and, keeping the gilding metal lengths parallel, wrap the wire around the spiral of silver.

silver wire.

Thin gilding metal wire.

2 Take care that the gilding metal wire is securely embedded between the twists throughout its length. When you reach the end, pass both ends of gilding metal through the fork in the silver and pull tight. Now check that the gilding metal is in contact with the silver throughout; if not, it is better to unwind and start again with a fresh piece of gilding metal.

3 If all is well, solder the gilding metal into place. Flux well, then place solder at each end of the work. As the flame passes down the work watch carefully to see that the solder melts either side of the gilding wire. Leave to soak in the acid pickle for up to an hour to remove any flux, then check for any gaps in the solder.

4 Saw off each end with a piercing saw and begin the forging process: begin by hammering the end until you have created a little fishtail, then work toward the middle to make an even, tapered flat. Turn the metal through 90 degrees and hammer the other end in exactly the same way. Use parallel-jawed pliers to hold the metal at right angles to the first forging.

As an alternative to the thin gilding metal stripe, you may prefer to have copper and silver stripes of equal width as for the twisted ring (see page 63).

5 When both ends are identical anneal, then continue forging, turning regularly until both sides have the same gradual taper with no suggestion of roundness between. At this stage you will find it best to hold the work with your fingers. Check regularly that the flat faces at each end of the pendant are at right angles to each other.

6 It may be necessary to use a file and emery boards for a completely smooth finish and to anneal the work part of the way through the forging process.

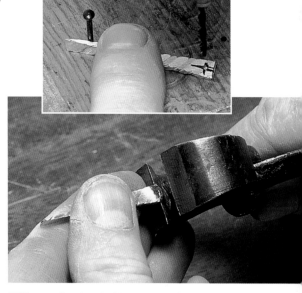

7 Square off each end with end cutters. Center punch and drill a 1/16 in (1.5 mm) hole.

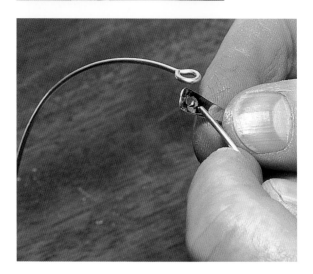

8 After polishing, the pendant is ready to hang on a leather thong or on a choker (see pages 44–45).

LESSON: **TYING THE KNOT**

Knots have been used in the making of jewelry since the earliest times, providing a rich source of practical inspiration for every kind of project. Apart from their obvious use as joining devices the history and symbolism associated with knots add an extra layer of meaning to jewelry work. Many of the complex forms seen in Celtic designs are derived from knots.

For a modeling material you need look no further than a ball of string. If you color some of the string with stain or ink, or use curtain cord in different colors, this will help you follow the construction of your models. It will also help you to appreciate the potential of combining different colored metals in your designs.

A knot made in wire usually looks most effective when not pulled tight, with spaces left between the wires. To help achieve this effect you may find a bodkin useful. This is a tool that has a point like a thick needle, polished smooth, with a wooden handle. A block of hardwood or metal with lots of small holes in a range of sizes will also be useful.

PROJECT 15 **FIGURE EIGHT KNOT RING**

YOU WILL NEED

- 4 x ³⁄₆₄ in (100 x 1.3 mm) round silver wire
- Vise
- Serrated-jawed pliers
- End cutters
- Hand file
- Bench peg
- Soldering equipment (see page 31)
- Bodkin (blunt thick needle) and block with holes
- Tapered mandrel
- Planishing hammer

| TECHNIQUES COVERED ● Cutting ● Soldering ● Planishing ● Forming ● Polishing |

The "lovers' knot" is commonly used, not only in jewelry making, and this figure eight motif often appears in heraldry as an emblem of faithful love. You may find it useful to practice tying the knot with string before moving on to wire.

1 Begin by forming a loop about a third of the way down the silver wire. Holding the loop in your left hand, with the short end of the wire on top, bend the long end over the short end, then down through the first loop.

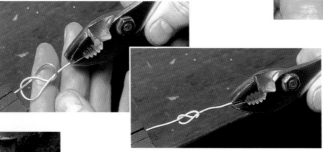

2 Hold the short end in a vise and pull the knot closed with serrated-jawed pliers. Remember not to pull the knot too tightly at this stage.

3 Trim off the surplus wire with end cutters, leaving the knot in the center of the wire. File the ends square through the hole in the bench peg. Bend the wire into a ring by hand and solder the join with easy solder. Place the ring face down over a hole in a block and push a bodkin into each gap in the knot until the spaces are as even as possible.

4 Planish the ring on a mandrel, beginning with the knot, to bed in the crossing points. A light touch is needed, just enough to remove the round appearance from the wire.

PROJECT 16 REEF KNOT BANGLE

YOU WILL NEED

- Vise
- Two lengths of round silver wire 7 x 1/16 in (180 x 1.5 mm)
- Soldering equipment (see page 31)
- Two 1/4 in (6 mm) steel rods
- Annealing equipment (see page 30)
- Parallel-jawed pliers
- Wood or metal block with holes in
- Polishing equipment (see page 34)
- Round former

TECHNIQUES COVERED ● Soldering ● Annealing ● Polishing

The reef knot is one of the oldest knots used in jewelry making. Two gold bangles identical to this one were found on the body of a young woman who lived in Egypt more than 4,000 years ago. The construction of this bangle is made easier by the closed loops that allow the force to be applied with steel rods. Drawing the knot together would be far more difficult if you had to grip the wire with pliers.

1 Solder the two ends of a length of silver wire to make a loop. Repeat with the other length. Pull the loops into shape using steel rods: with the join against one of the steel rods, pull the other end of the loop against a rod gripped in a vise.

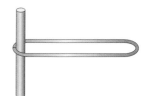

Position the join against one of the rods.

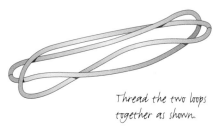

Thread the two loops together as shown.

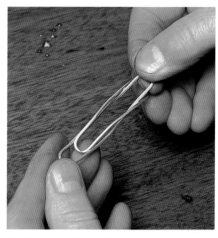

2 Now thread the two loops together; you will need to bend both and widen one end of each loop. The joins must be at either end of the bangle, clear of the knot.

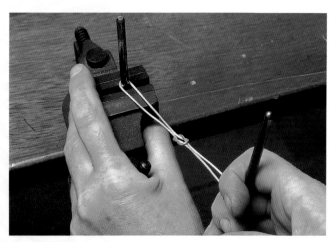

3 Gently pull the knot into place using the steel rods.

4 Carefully place four pallions of solder in the folds between the wires. Now solder the knot together.

5 After soldering, anneal the rest of the bangle. Now use parallel-jawed pliers to pinch each end of the loop around one of the rods, creating loops at each end of the bangle. This task will be a little easier if you steady the rod in a hole in a piece of wood or metal.

6 Hold the work against a piece of wood and polish it. Then bend it into the required shape by pressing it around a former.

PROJECT 17 REEF KNOT RING WITH STONE

YOU WILL NEED

- 7 x ½ in (180 x 1mm) round silver wire
- Hand file
- Bench peg
- End cutters
- Soldering equipment (see page 31)
- Steel plate with holes
- Two ¹⁵⁄₆₄ in (6 mm) steel rods
- ¹³⁄₆₄ in (5 mm) steel rod
- ⅝ x ⁵⁄₆₄ x ¹⁄₆₄ in (16 x 2 x 0.25 mm) strip of bezel silver
- Tapered mandrel
- ³⁵⁄₆₄ x ½ in (14 x 1 mm) round silver wire
- Cabochon
- Parallel-jawed pliers

TECHNIQUES COVERED ● Cutting ● Soldering ● Forming ● Polishing

The knot in this project is the setting for a small cabochon, the final assembly of the ring presenting a somewhat delicate soldering challenge. A cabochon is a smooth, domed stone, usually round or oval in shape. A bezel is the thin band of metal that holds the cabochon in place, while the bearer is that part of the jewelry piece on which the cabochon rests.

1 Begin by cutting the ½ in (1 mm) wire into two equal lengths. File the ends square on the hole in the bench peg and form them into two loops by soldering the ends of each loop together. Thread the two loops together into a loose reef knot (see Steps 2–3, page 70). Place a ¹³⁄₆₄ in (5 mm) steel rod into a hole in a steel plate, thread the knot onto the rod and pull tight, using two ¹⁵⁄₆₄ in (6 mm) steel rods as levers.

2 Solder the knot using four tiny pallions. Form the strip of bezel silver into a ring and solder it together. To make it fit the cabochon, place it over a hole in the steel plate and hammer a tapered mandrel through it until you have stretched it to the correct size. Check it regularly for size against the cabochon to avoid stretching it too much.

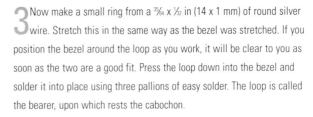

3 Now make a small ring from a ³⁵⁄₆₄ x ½ in (14 x 1 mm) of round silver wire. Stretch this in the same way as the bezel was stretched. If you position the bezel around the loop as you work, it will be clear to you as soon as the two are a good fit. Press the loop down into the bezel and solder it into place using three pallions of easy solder. The loop is called the bearer, upon which rests the cabochon.

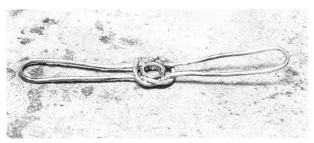

4 Open out the knot using the mandrel over a hole, as you did with the bezel and the bearer, until the setting is a precise fit. It must be possible to pick up the whole work by either end without the setting dropping out. Solder the setting into the knot with as much of the bezel showing above the knot wires as possible. This is best done with the setting upside down.

5 When the setting has been soldered into the knot it is time to form the two wire loops into a ring. Snip the loops open and straighten out all four wires.

6 Cut to length and file the ends flat in the bench peg.

As you solder the back of the ring make sure you do not melt the delicate setting.

7 Solder the two joins together separately. Bring the first join together with your fingers, solder it, then bend it aside and repeat the process with the other wire. Push the ring onto the tapered mandrel and press the two wires together with parallel-jawed pliers. To set the stone see page 110.

LESSON: JEWELRY WITHOUT SOLDER

Soldering is without doubt a most important part of jewelry making. There can be few more rewarding sights than that of molten metal flowing around a join, and mastery of the soldering torch is in many ways the key to success when making jewelry.

However, many people find the process difficult, including the very young, the partially sighted, and those who for varying reasons find the heat that is required for soldering too intense. The equipment is also rather costly. A heat source of some kind is necessary, however, if only for the essential process of annealing, and a kitchen cooker or camping stove will serve both processes well. Jump rings are usually soldered, but if you use thicker wire and work harden the ring by repeated bending, there is no need to resort to soldering. The projects in this section show you the many ways in which you can make beautiful jewelry without solder.

PROJECT 18 SILVER BROOCH

YOU WILL NEED
- 12 x ¾₄ in (300 x 1.2 mm) round silver wire
- Hand file
- Round-nosed pliers
- End cutters
- Bench peg
- Planishing hammer and domed stake
- Polishing equipment (see page 34)

TECHNIQUES COVERED ● Cutting ● Planishing ● Polishing

The basic construction of this brooch provides an opportunity to try out a range of designs. The main constraint is that the wire must not overlap itself. Thicker wire can be used which will add some rigidity to the structure, though you will probably have to file the pin down to prevent too large a hole being made in the wearer's clothes.

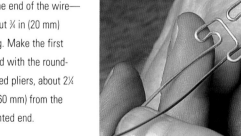

1 Begin by filing a point on one end of the wire—make it a gradual taper about ¾ in (20 mm) long. Make the first bend with the round-nosed pliers, about 2¼ in (60 mm) from the pointed end.

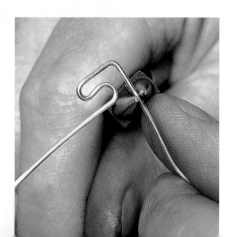

2 Continue bending, keeping the straight sections as short as possible. Different parts of the wire may touch but must not overlap.

3 When the last bend is made, the remaining wire must be at right angles to the pin and the pin must be ²⁵⁄₆₄ in (10 mm) longer than the bent section. Trim the end to about ¹⁹⁄₃₂ in (15 mm) longer than your chosen design.

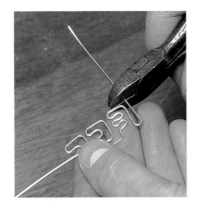

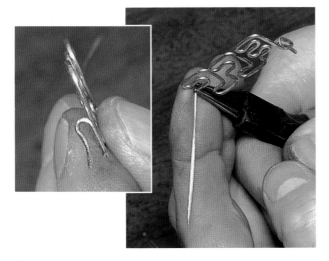

4 Now planish the piece, with the pin hammered lightly all round to harden it and make it straight. Striking the outside of each bend will help to preserve its shape and vary the wire's width. Planishing will stretch the design so used round-nosed pliers to make any adjustments.

5 Use the pliers to bend up the right-angled end to form the keeper, and bend the pin over to engage with it. Polish the brooch on a polishing pad with powdered rouge.

Here are some other suggested designs. Sketch a few ideas of your own and make models in thin copper wire before you begin to work in silver.

PROJECT 19 SCROLL PENDANT WITH BEAD

YOU WILL NEED

- 8 x ¾₄ in (200 x 1.3 mm) round silver wire
- Hand file
- Annealing equipment (see page 30)
- Bench peg
- Parallel-jawed pliers
- Ruler
- Round-nosed pliers
- Planishing hammer and domed stake
- Bead for pendant
- 6¼ x ¾₄ (160 x 1.1 mm) round silver wire
- Two earring hooks and jump rings (see page 120)
- Two beads for earrings

TECHNIQUES COVERED ● Annealing ● Planishing

This double scroll pendant, consisting of a large scroll doubled over a smaller one, gives the impression of musical notation. You can vary the length or thickness of the wire in order to change the character of the finished project.

1 Begin by filing a taper on each end of the silver wire and annealing the wire. Then form a scroll on one end (see Steps 2–3, pages 56–57). Continue this scroll until you have used up slightly more than half the wire. Making a model in copper first will help you decide on precise dimensions, as well as whether the scroll should be open or more densely formed.

2 Use parallel-jawed pliers to bend the end of the scroll sharply so that the unused wire lines up with the center of the scroll.

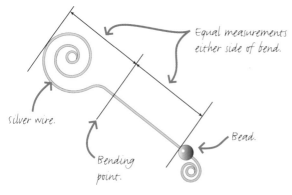

Equal measurements either side of bend.

Silver wire.

Bending point.

Bead.

Hold the straight section with parallel-jawed pliers as you bend the small scroll into line.

3 Planish the scroll and about 1³⁄₁₆ in (30 mm) of the straight section. Thread on a bead and form the second, smaller scroll at the other end of the wire. At this point check that enough straight wire remains between the two scrolls to allow the large scroll to be bent over to meet the bead, leaving a short section at the top of the earring, above the large scroll.

4 Grip the wire at the bending point with round-nosed pliers. Bend each side over, a little at a time, to ensure that the large scroll finishes on top of the bead. To make matching earrings use a 6¼ x ³⁄₆₄ in (160 x 1.1 mm) silver wire. Proceed as for the pendant. Use about half the wire for the large scroll. Remember to thread on the bead before making the second scroll. Make each stage of both earrings at the same time as this will help you to make them identical.

5 Attach each earring to an earring hook using a jump ring. Bend the jump rings back and forth a few times to make them hard. The pendant is hung directly onto a chain or cord without the need for a jump ring.

PROJECT 20 SCROLL AND SPIRAL BRACELET

YOU WILL NEED
- Five lengths of 4¾ x ³⁄₆₄ in (120 x 1.2 mm) round silver wire
- Annealing equipment (see page 30)
- Parallel-jawed pliers
- Hand file
- Bench peg
- Former, such as a strip of metal ¹³⁄₆₄ x ¹⁄₁₆ in (5 x 1.5 mm)
- Permanent marker pen
- Planishing hammer and flat stake
- Polishing equipment (see page 34)
- Five lengths of 6 x ¹⁄₁₆ in (150 x 1.5 mm) round silver wire
- Jump ring
- Round-nosed pliers
- ⁵⁄₆₄ in (2 mm) diameter metal rod former
- End cutters

TECHNIQUES COVERED • Annealing • Planishing • Polishing • Cutting

This silver bracelet is made of five S-shaped scrolls that are connected to each other by four scroll-ended spirals. The secret of its assembly lies in carrying out each stage in the correct order.

1 Start by making the four connecting spirals. Taper each end of the four 4¾ x ³⁄₆₄ in (120 x 1.1 mm) wires. Anneal the wires and mark the center of each one.

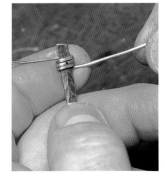

2 Wrap one wire around a ⁵⁄₃₂ x ¹⁄₁₆ in (4 x 1.5 mm) metal former, starting with the center mark against the middle.

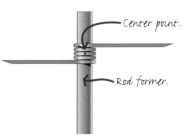

Center point.
Rod former.

3 When you can see five wire wraps it is time to scroll the ends (see Steps 2–3, pages 56–57). Use a closed scroll and try to make them as nearly identical as possible.

4 Planish each scroll on the edge of a flat stake. The spiral can be lightly planished with the former in place, but take care not to hammer this too hard as it may get stuck on the former. Polish each little spiral now; it is much easier to polish each element separately before assembly. Repeat Steps 2–4 with the remaining three wires.

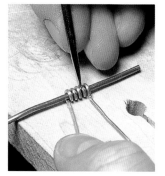

5 Begin making the five scrolls from 6 x ³⁄₆₄ in (150 x 1.3 mm) silver wire. Taper each end and anneal before forming the first scroll. Stop when you have 3 in (75 mm) of straight wire remaining. Planish and polish each scroll without touching the straight section. Begin assembly by threading two of the little spirals onto one of the partially completed scrolls; push them as far around the scroll as you can. Make sure the planished side is on top on each component. Form the other end of the first scroll; planish and polish it.

6 The second spiral can now be moved to the other end of the scroll, leaving one at each end. Now thread on the second partly finished scroll and continue the process until all, except the final scroll, are complete and joined. As the bracelet gets longer, take care not to allow the finished end anywhere near the polishing mop.

7 Make the double hook fastener by winding the remaining 6 x ³⁄₆₄ in (150 x 1.3 mm) wire around the ⁵⁄₆₄ in (2 mm) rod former. Leave about 1⅛ in (28 mm) of straight wire at the beginning. Make five coils, then bend the remaining straight sections so that they face in the same direction and are in line with the coil's center. Trim to 1 in (25 mm). Round off and polish the ends. Arrange the wire so that the coils are evenly spaced, and the wires in line with the last gap in the scroll.

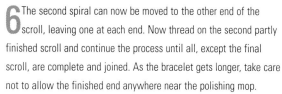

Double hook fastener.

8 Bend the ends upward, then over, to complete the hooks. Thread the hook onto the last scroll, form the final S-scroll, planish and polish. Bend each scroll slightly, to improve the fit of the bracelet.

LESSON: MAKING AND USING A BENDING JIG

A bending jig is easy to make, and once made, it can be used to create a range of jewelry pieces, all with a common theme. It will enable you to make identical earrings and other matching units with little difficulty.

This jig is made of perforated steel sheets bolted together so that the holes in the sheets line up with each other. The pins are steel pop rivets. However, a piece of steel mesh fastened to a piece of plywood and the hard round nails used for picture hanging will do equally well.

YOU WILL NEED

- Two sheets of perforated steel, 4 x 2¾ in (100 x 70 mm)
- Hand file and emery cloth
- Electric drill and ⁹⁄₆₄ in (3.2 mm) drill bit
- Four 1 x ⅛ in (25 x 3 mm) bolts with 20 nuts
- Fifty ⅛ in (3 mm) steel pop rivets

1 Round off the corners of both perforated sheets with a hand file and emery cloth. Use the electric drill to drill a hole in each corner.

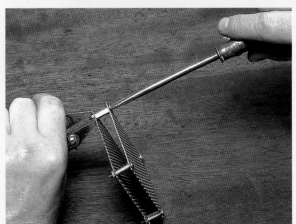

2 Assemble the two halves using the nuts and bolts. Several nuts can be used to create the space between the two sheets of steel. The spacers used here are the metal inserts from electrical junction boxes.

3 Hold the jig securely in a vise.

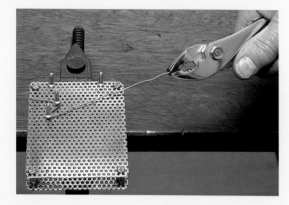

4 An alternative method of making a bending jig is to drill the holes in a solid steel plate. The plate shown here is ¹⁵⁄₆₄ in (6 mm) thick. Drilling the holes is time-consuming, but you can mark them out by using a piece of perforated steel as a template and taping it to the steel plate before you start drilling.

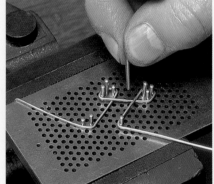

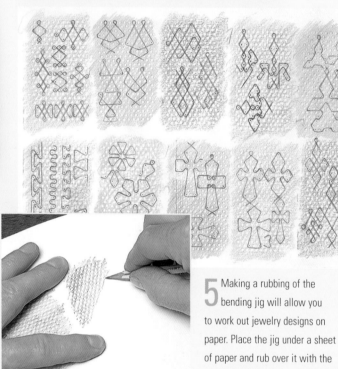

5 Making a rubbing of the bending jig will allow you to work out jewelry designs on paper. Place the jig under a sheet of paper and rub over it with the side of a pencil or crayon.

The jewelry pieces shown here demonstrate just some of the possibilities presented by the bending jig.

PROJECT 21 BENDING JIG PENDANT AND EARRINGS

YOU WILL NEED

- 32 x ¾ in (800 x 1.2 mm) round silver wire
- Bending jig
- Vise
- Engineer's pliers
- Nail
- Annealing equipment (see page 30)
- Flattening device (see page 15)
- Soldering equipment (see page 31)
- Planishing hammer and flat stake
- End cutters
- Polishing equipment (see page 34)

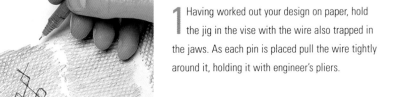

TECHNIQUES COVERED ● Bending ● Annealing ● Soldering ● Planishing ● Polishing

The designs of this pendant and earrings are near identical, but you may prefer to use slightly thinner wire for the earrings or making subtle changes to the pendant design.

1 Having worked out your design on paper, hold the jig in the vise with the wire also trapped in the jaws. As each pin is placed pull the wire tightly around it, holding it with engineer's pliers.

2 Pulling the wire around a nail at the end will help keep the design in place when you remove the pins. Use pliers to remove the pins.

3 After annealing, flatten the work using the flattening device, then solder the overlapping wires to each other. You can now trim off the loose ends with end cutters and lightly planish the work. Polishing is best done with polishing pads, but if you are using a polishing machine hold the work firmly against a piece of wood.

PROJECT 22 BENDING JIG RING

YOU WILL NEED
- 16 x ½ in (400 x 1 mm) round silver wire
- Bending jig
- Wire cutters
- Hand file
- Soldering equipment (see page 31)
- Planishing hammer
- Tapered mandrel
- Polishing equipment (see page 34)

TECHNIQUES COVERED ● Bending ● Soldering ● Planishing ● Polishing

This ring demonstrates the unexpected effects that can come from experimenting with the bending jig. The light planishing has created subtle curves reminiscent of Art Nouveau style.

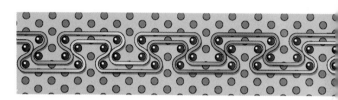

1 Begin by forming two sections of wire on the bending jig, each with four small dovetails, leaving a long straight section at either end. It is important to make the two rings identical, and to ensure that each of the four sections of each ring are the same, including the section containing the join.

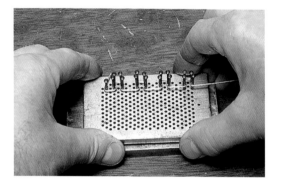

2 File the ends of the two lengths of bent wire until the section containing the join is the same length as the other sections of the ring. Join up the two rings with easy solder. There will be some distortion at this stage but this will easily be corrected when you thread the ring onto the tapered mandrel.

3 Planish the ring carefully, using light hammer blows; it will be easy to distort this thin wire. After polishing, fit the two rings together. Further planishing may be necessary after the rings have been fitted together.

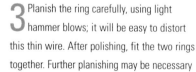

ETCHING

Etching is the process of eroding metal by chemical action. Parts of the metal in question are covered with a stopping-out medium called a resist. This can be a bitumastic- or pitch-based paint, a permanent marker pen, a rub-down transfer, or a self-adhesive label. When the work is immersed in the etchant, those areas left exposed are eaten away, leaving the protected or stopped-out parts unaffected. As etching is a fairly gentle process, it can be used to add designs to areas, such as the insides of rings, that would otherwise be difficult to reach.

The etching of precious metals requires the use of hydrochloric and nitric acids as etchants. Copper, brass, and bronze can be etched using ferric chloride, a less hazardous solution and a more suitable introduction to the technique. Nickel silver etches well, and old cutlery with all its silver plating worn off is a cheap source of material for practice. Using base metals allows you a more adventurous approach as only by much trial and error can you learn to fully appreciate the creative possibilities offered by the etching process.

Etching solution in jar in plastic tray to protect against splashes.

LESSON: STOPPING OUT AND ETCHING

YOU WILL NEED

- Copper, brass, or bronze sheet
- Acid pickle
- Adhesive tape
- Etch resists for stopping out, such as permanent marker pen, rub-down transfers, and self-adhesive parcel labels
- Penknife
- Burnisher
- Etchant (ferric chloride)
- Plastic tray
- Insulated wire

PERMANENT PEN

Polish the work piece and clean it thoroughly, either with a spirit or in an acid pickle, before fastening it to a strip of adhesive tape. This allows the work to be held firmly while you work on it, and removes the need to touch the metal surface with your fingers. The tape also provides a means by which you can suspend the work in the etchant. Use a permanent pen to draw the design on the metal and a border to protect the metal edges, which are especially vulnerable to the action of the etchant. The reverse is, of course, protected by the adhesive tape. You can correct mistakes by carefully scraping away the unwanted ink with a penknife; the little scratches will be eroded by the etching process.

STOPPING OUT—RUB-DOWN TRANSFERS

If you use rub-down transfers, they must be firmly pressed down using the backing paper and a burnisher.

ADHESIVE LABELS

Also use a burnisher to ensure that adhesive label designs are firmly fixed to the surface of the metal.

SAFETY CONSIDERATIONS

- Etching chemicals can be dangerous when inhaled and can cause serious burns when they come into contact with the skin. Always wear protective gloves, a respirator, and goggles when working with them and ensure that your workplace is well-ventilated.
- Etchant in the form of ferric chloride stains clothing, bench, or table tops so be sure to protect your clothes and surrounding work area.

THE ETCHING PROCESS

Etchants (ferric chloride) often come in the form of pellets that dissolve in warm water and the solution can still be used quite successfully when cold. Working in a well-ventilated area and wearing protective gloves, goggles, and a mask, mix the etchant in a strong, non-metallic container placed inside a plastic tray with a bowl of rinsing water alongside, following the manufacturer's instructions. Hang your metal piece from a length of insulated wire and suspend it in the solution. The length of time the work remains in the etchant depends on the strength of the solution, the depth of the bite required, and the type of resist used. Transfers and permanent pen marks tend to degrade over time. Adhesive labels allow for a longer etching time and therefore a deeper bite. Check the work every five or ten minutes by pulling it out of the solution.

PROJECT 23 BRONZE RING

YOU WILL NEED
- 2½ x ⁵⁄₁₆ x ½ in (65 x 8 x 0.8 mm) bronze ring
- Self-adhesive parcel labels
- Scissors
- Etching equipment (see page 84)
- Soldering torch
- 2²³⁄₆₄ x ⁵⁄₁₆ x ¹⁄₆₄ in (60 x 8 x 0.5 mm) silver strip
- Dividers
- 45-degree punch

TECHNIQUES COVERED ● Etching ● Cutting

This bronze ring demonstrates the effectiveness of the adhesive label method of stopping out. The etchant (ferric chloride) bites deep into the metal, transforming it completely.

1 Clean a bronze ring thoroughly in acid pickle. Cut strips of adhesive label about ¹⁄₁₆ in (1.5 mm) wide and wind them around the ring. Start at the join as the solder will not be affected by the etchant and, if left exposed, will leave a sharp ridge. Continue until you have covered about half the area of the ring.

2 Immerse the ring in the etchant for about an hour, hanging it by a short length of insulated wire. Allow the ring to be suspended midway down the container. Do not be tempted to leave it in for too long—you could find nothing left but the adhesive strips. When the depth of bite is to your liking, rinse the ring thoroughly in water.

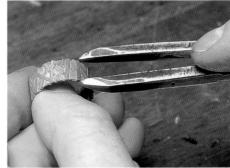

3 Remove the stopping-out strips by burning them off with the soldering torch, then leave them to clean in the acid pickle. Next, make the ring's silver liner. Set dividers to the width of the ring and mark out and cut a strip of ¹⁄₆₄ in (0.5 mm)-thick silver (see page 23). You can make the the liner ¹³⁄₆₄ in (5 mm) shorter than the etched ring and stretch it to fit by planishing. Secure the liner into the ring using a 45-degree punch.

PROJECT 24 SPOON PENDANT

YOU WILL NEED
- Nickel silver teaspoon
- Annealing equipment (see page 30)
- Jeweler's shears
- Acid pickle
- Piercing saw
- Planishing hammer
- Domed stake
- Fine sable brush
- Small lump of pitch or tar
- Paraffin
- Etching equipment (see page 84)
- Electric drill and 1/16 in (1.5 mm) and 5/64 in (2 mm) bits

TECHNIQUES COVERED ● Annealing ● Planishing ● Polishing ● Etching ● Drilling

The charm of this nickel pendant is that a second glance is required to establish that it began life as a spoon. The etched design, together with the little hangings, provide plenty of scope for the imagination.

1 Anneal the spoon, then snip off the end of the spoon's bowl using jeweler's shears, and planish it from the back on a domed stake. Hammer a flat on the neck to allow for a hole to be drilled for hanging.

2 Polish and thoroughly clean the bowl in acid pickle. Holding the work by the handle, paint on your design with a fine sable brush and pitch or tar, using paraffin as a solvent.

3 Try to apply an even coating of pitch. Remember to cover the edges and to make allowance for the holes along the bottom edge. Mask off the reverse with adhesive tape, before etching until the desired bite is achieved.

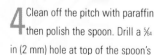

4 Clean off the pitch with paraffin then polish the spoon. Drill a 5/64 in (2 mm) hole at top of the spoon's bowl and three 1/16 in (1.5 mm) holes at the bottom of the bowl from which to attach scrolls and beads. Finally saw off the handle and fit a jump ring to the first hole for a chain.

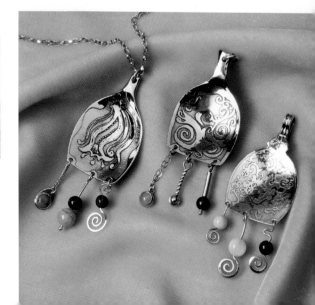

PROJECT 25 **BELT BUCKLE**

YOU WILL NEED
- 2¾ x 2 x ½₂ in (70 x 50 x 1 mm) brass or bronze strip
- Jeweler's shears
- Hand file
- Emery boards of varying grades
- Rolled-hide mallet
- Sandbag or telephone book
- Planishing hammer and domed stake
- Etching equipment (see page 84)
- 4¾ x ⁵⁄₆₄ in (120 x 2 mm) round copper wire
- Soldering equipment (see page 31) plus extra soldering torch
- End cutters
- Spirit such as nail varnish remover

TECHNIQUES COVERED • Cutting • Forming • Planishing • Etching • Cutting • Soldering

The belt buckle, with a large blank area, makes an ideal subject for an etching project. In this design the belt is not permanently fixed, so there is no need to apply rivets to the leather belt.

1 Choose a shape for your buckle and cut it out with shears. Finish the edges with a file and emery boards.

2 After annealing, hollow the metal slightly with a mallet on a sandbag—a pile of newspapers or a telephone book makes a satisfactory substitute for a sandbag.

3 Planish the metal, starting in the middle and working toward the outside, taking care to cover every part of the metal's surface.

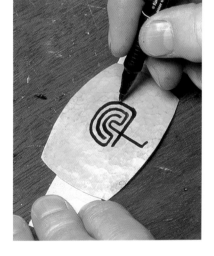

4 After cleaning in acid pickle, draw the design on with a permanent marker pen. Be sure to get a good coating of ink on the metal; tapping gently with the point on the work will sometimes help the ink to flow.

5 Scrape off any minor errors with a penknife. If you make any serious mistakes do not be afraid to clean the whole lot off with spirit and start again.

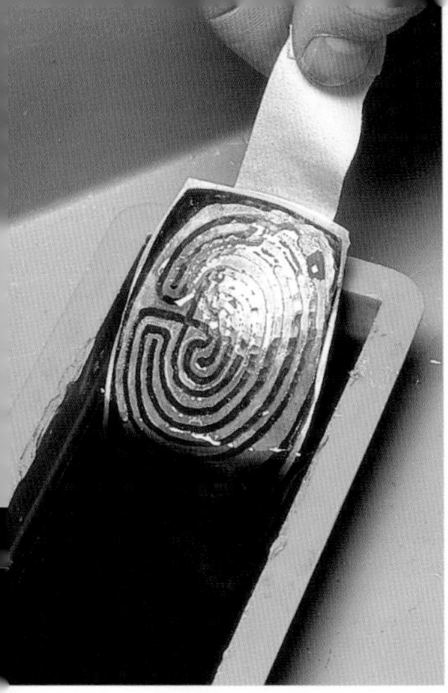

6 Stop out the reverse with adhesive tape and place the metal in the etchant for about an hour, checking regularly that your pen marks have not lifted.

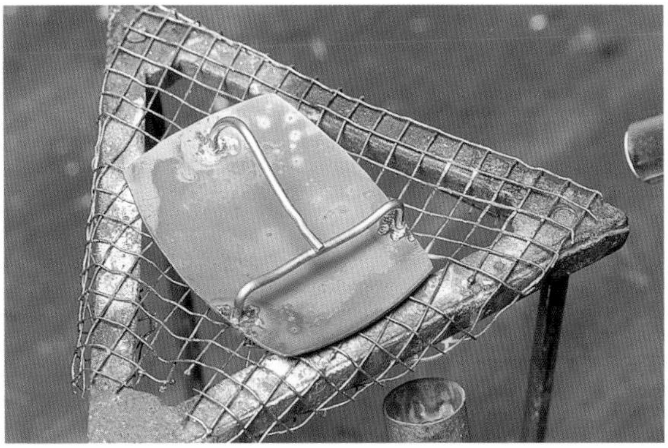

7 The loop and post must now be soldered on in two stages. First cut off a $2\frac{23}{64}$ in (60 mm) length of copper wire. File both ends square and bend into shape. Solder the remainder of the wire to the middle of the loop; use hard solder for this join, which will lessen the chance of it melting during the next stage of the operation. This creates a three-legged form that must be fitted into place, with the post about $\frac{25}{64}$ in (10 mm) from one end and the loop about $\frac{19}{32}$ in (15 mm) from the other. With the fluxed work positioned on top of a tripod and three pallions against each join, solder the two wires into place. Use two torches, one on top and one underneath the tripod.

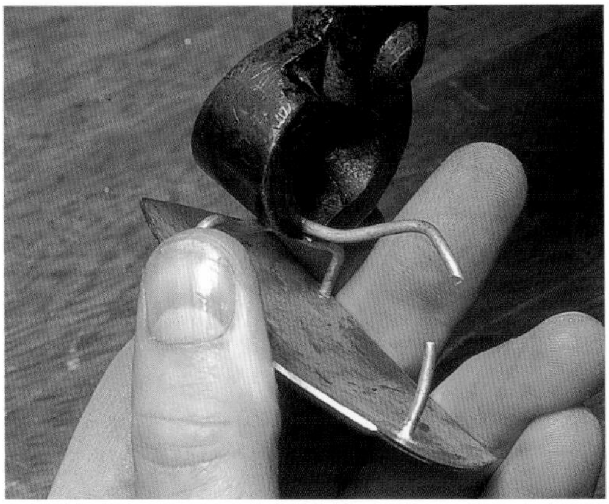

8 Soldered work of this kind leaves a good deal of oxide and spent flux. This will need a long soak in the acid pickle to remove it. When the work is clean, cut away the middle section of wire between the loop and the post; this should be about $\frac{19}{32}$ in (15 mm) long.

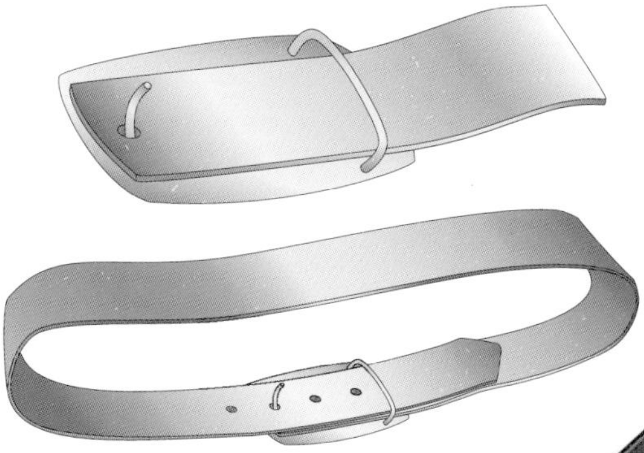

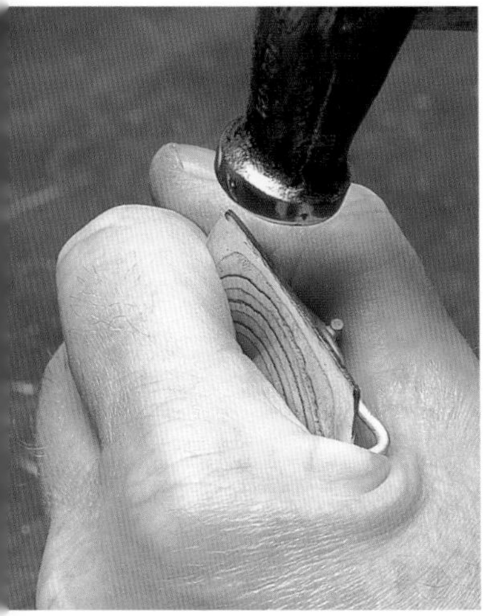

9 Bend both pieces of wire back and forth repeatedly. This will make them harder after the soldering process. The remainder of the metal remains soft and further planishing of the face is out of the question. After smoothing the edge with a file and emery boards, planish all round with the work held firmly in the fist. This process has the effect of hardening and thickening the edge, making the whole piece more rigid.

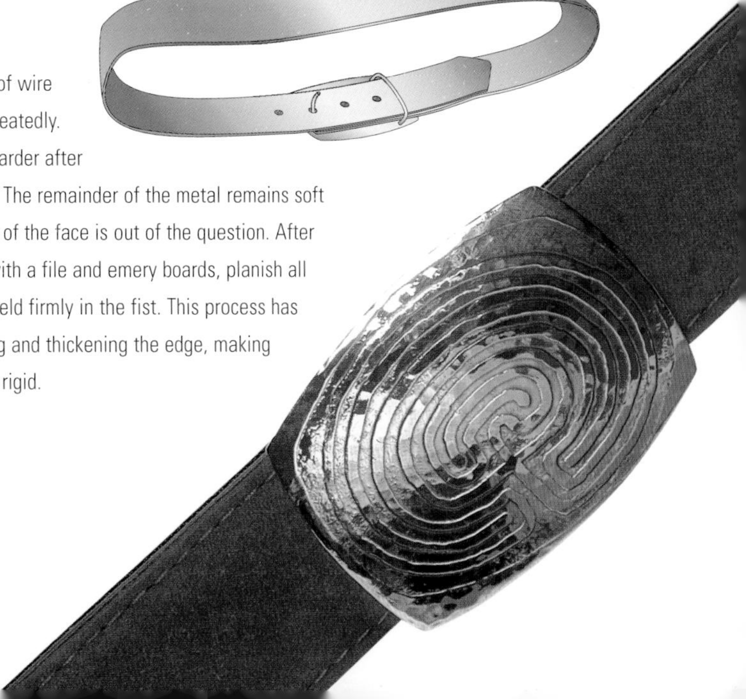

MELTING AND FUSING

One of the most common ways in which disaster can strike the jewelry maker is when his or her work is melted by the soldering torch. Both silver and gold will melt very readily, as will brass and bronze to a lesser extent. Silver is particularly prized for its flow properties, which is why it is the most important constituent in many industrial melting alloys. Only by experience can you learn, and the best way to learn how not to melt silver is to melt it, regularly and often. As you observe the melting you will come to recognize the condition, color, and surface texture of metal that is about to melt.

You can create some interesting effects when silver is melted. You will require a certain mindset for this kind of work—disaster is just around the corner, so it is as well to be prepared for the worst. Sometimes the work turns up a pleasant and unexpected surprise; at other times you will find you have created a formless blob. The most important end to this kind of work is the invaluable experience it provides and, however it ends, you can always turn it into solder.

LESSON: BALLING UP

SILVER BEADS

1 Take a scrap of silver and heat it on a piece of charcoal or a firebrick. Touch it lightly with the end of a borax cone; this will deposit enough flux to prevent oxide forming when you heat the metal. Now heat the silver until it melts into a little bead, rather like a drop of water on a waxy surface. This is known as balling up.

2 Make a collection of beads for use in projects such as the twisted bangle on page 64. Very small pieces will melt into perfectly round balls.

YOU WILL NEED
- Scrap of silver
- Soldering equipment (see page 31)
- Round silver wire
- Round-nosed pliers
- End cutters

BALLING UP WIRE ENDS

3 The ends of wires can be balled up, though this takes a little more practice—it is all too easy to damage the structure of the metal alongside the ball so that it subsequently breaks. The ball will sometimes form off center and if you make it too big it can drop off the end of the wire. The solution to all these problems lies in practice. Take a length of silver wire. Hold it with pliers about 2 in (50 mm) from the end. Heat it, touch it on the borax cone, and then put it back in the flame until a ball forms on the end.

4 Discard the unsatisfactory results and snip off the good ones with about 1½–2 in (40–50 mm) of straight wire to use, among other things, as bead hangers on the spoon pendant (see page 87).

PROJECT 26 BALLED-UP RING

YOU WILL NEED

- 3½ x 3⁄64 in (90 x 1.3 mm) round silver wire
- Soldering equipment (see page 31)
- Parallel-jawed pliers
- Planishing hammer
- Tapered mandrel

TECHNIQUES COVERED ● Balling Up ● Soldering ● Planishing

This little ring provides good practice in balling up wire. You could use brass wire to practice as this will melt in much the same way as silver does. If a ring is slightly smaller than the size required, it is always possible to enlarge it by planishing.

1 Ball up both ends of the wire (see page 90) until you have reduced the 3½ in (90 mm) length to about 2¾ in (70 mm). Try to make the two balls as near equal in size as possible.

2 Bend the two ends so that they touch just behind the balls. Solder the wires together at the point where they meet using a generous amount of easy solder. You may need to leave your work in the acid pickle for some time to dissolve the spent flux from the balling-up process.

3 After straightening the shank (back of the ring) with parallel-jawed pliers, planish the back and sides of the ring on a tapered mandrel. Take care not to damage the balls as you work on the shoulder.

YOU WILL NEED

- Jeweler's shears
- 6 x ½ in (150 x 0.8 mm) round silver wire
- 3⅛ x ⁵⁄₁₆ x ½ in (80 x 8 x 0.8 mm) silver strip
- Planishing hammer and flat stake
- Soldering equipment (see page 31)
- Binding wire
- Bench peg
- Piercing saw
- Rolled-hide mallet
- Tapered mandrel
- Emery board
- Penknife
- Polishing equipment (see page 34)
- 3⅛ x ⁵⁄₁₆ x ¹⁄₆₄ in (80 x 8 x 0.8 mm) bronze strip
- 2¾ x ⁵⁄₁₆ x ¹⁄₆₄ in (65 x 8 x 0.5 mm) silver strip
- Vise

PROJECT 27 SILVER AND BRONZE FUSED RINGS

> **TECHNIQUES COVERED** ● Cutting ● Planishing ● Soldering ● Polishing ● Forming

Fusing is the joining of metals by means of heat without the use of solder. The metal melts only on the surface, leaving the core unchanged. Silver and gold are particularly suited to fusing. The high temperatures and careful control required make fusing a good way of practicing the use of the soldering torch. Fusing is an unpredictable process, so make your designs random; precise patterns may be difficult to achieve by this method. The distinctive texture on the surface of this fused silver ring provides a sharp contrast to the highly polished edges.

1 Begin by cutting the silver wire into small pieces. These can be any shape, but small enough to make an interesting pattern. For fusing to be successful there must be good surface contact between the metals, so flatten both the blank silver strip and the wire pieces with a planishing hammer. Coat all the parts with flux and arrange them on the surface of the blank, which itself rests on a piece of binding wire.

2 Start fusing by directing the flame along the work, starting at the front and moving on as each section fuses.

Unfused pieces.

Look out for the shiny fillet of metal at the point where the metals join; this is an indication that the metal is molten.

3 When the work has been thoroughly soaked in the acid pickle to remove all traces of spent flux, examine it carefully and saw off the least effective sections.

4 Bend the blank to shape using the bench peg rather than pliers to avoid any damage to the fused surface. Solder the blank closed from the inside to prevent getting solder on the fused surface.

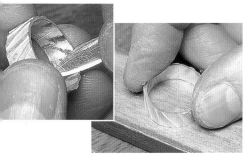

5 Make the ring round on a tapered mandrel with a mallet. Polish the edges of the fused ring to a high sheen to provide a sharp contrast to the texture on the face. Finish the ring using a file, then finer and finer emery boards, until the edge is smooth enough to polish without risk of rounding it off. A penknife held flat against the inside of the edge is the best way to remove the uncomfortable burr.

BRONZE RING

6 Fusing is particularly effective when different metals are involved. Here the bronze strip has been used as the base with little silver chevrons fused onto it.

7 To prevent the bronze staining the skin and to add interest to the piece you can line it with a thin strip of silver. Make the liner from the 1/64 in (0.5 mm) thick silver strip. The liner should be approximately 1/8 in (3 mm) shorter in length than the ring so that it can be stretched to a tight fit. Planish very gently, and try to create parallel stripes with your hammer. This is an indication that you are hammering the surface evenly. Keep trying the liner in the bronze ring—if you do stretch it too far you can file it down; the file marks will not show.

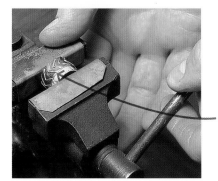

8 When a tight or force fit is achieved you can squeeze the liner into place in a vise.

There should be no need to solder the liner into place provided you have made it a good fit.

PROJECT 28 FUSED BRONZE CROSS

YOU WILL NEED

- 2 x 1½ x ⅟₃₂ in (50 x 40 x 1 mm) bronze strip
- Punch and die
- Heavy hammer
- Ruler
- Permanent marker pen
- Jeweler's shears
- 4 x ³⁄₆₄ in (100 x 1.3 mm) silver wire
- Planishing hammer and flat stake
- Soldering equipment (see page 31)
- Electric drill with ⅛ in (3 mm) bit
- Center punch
- Wood block
- Polishing equipment (see page 34)

TECHNIQUES COVERED ● Cutting ● Drilling ● Polishing

This simple cross is embellished with fused silver pieces. As the bronze tarnishes, the silver shows up more clearly. The punch and die provide a more effective means than drilling of making holes in the metal, and the cross is easy to cut once the four holes have been made.

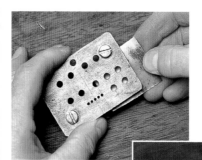

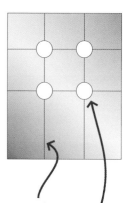

Guide lines for cutting cross shape.

Punch holes.

1 Place the bronze strip into the die, tighten the screws and punch out the four holes with a punch and heavy hammer.

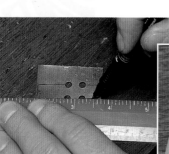

2 Using the holes as a guide, mark out the cross with a permanent marker pen. Cut out the corners using jeweler's shears and trim the ends of each arm of the cross. When cutting out the corners, take care not to over-reach with the shears and snip the far side of the hole.

3 Cut about nine small lengths of silver wire to fuse to the cross. Flatten the bronze and silver pieces to ensure a good contact between them.

4 Flux both the silver and bronze parts thoroughly. Position the silver pieces on the bronze cross and apply the heat. Start at the front, and move the flame up as the pieces fuse. Look for the telltale sign of bright molten metal at the border between silver and bronze, then move on rapidly to the next piece.

POINTS TO NOTE

● If you allow the heat to remain too long on one section, the silver will flow out onto the surrounding metal. If this happens, do not abandon the project. Instead, reheat all the silver pieces so that the whole area is covered in a thin coating of silver. Then try fusing more silver pieces on the other side of the cross.

5 Mark the position of the hole for the necklace. Mark the hole with a permanent marker pen, then center punch and drill it on a wood block using the ⅛ in (3 mm) drill bit. Hold the work down with your fingers; your nail will prevent the work spinning round if the drill should jam. Polish to finish.

YOU WILL NEED

- Scraps of silver
- Soldering equipment (see page 31)
- End cutters
- Scraps of copper
- Polishing equipment (see page 34)
- Scraps of copper or brass
- Hammer and steel plate
- Coarse emery paper
- Rolling mill
- Annealing equipment (see page 30)

PROJECT 29 SILVER SCRAPS FUSED PENDANT

| TECHNIQUES COVERED ● Planishing ● Polishing |

Fusing pieces of silver to each other rather than to a base can offer good opportunities for creating jewelry. The initial arrangement of the scraps and the way the heat is applied can allow you some control over the finished product. If you are making a pendant, for instance, try to incorporate the hanging device into the fusing.

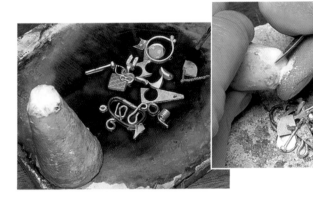

1 Begin by covering all the silver scraps with flux, then use them to make an arrangement of your choice, incorporating the hanging device (a closed loop, for example) into the design. Heat the arrangement using the soldering torch then add more flux by scraping it off the borax cone as a powder and onto the metal. It is important to do this when the silver is hot to ensure that the flux melts onto the silver and is not blown away by the flame.

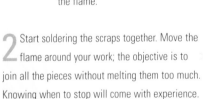

2 Start soldering the scraps together. Move the flame around your work; the objective is to join all the pieces without melting them too much. Knowing when to stop will come with experience.

3 Any sharp points that have stubbornly refused to melt away can be snipped off with end cutters. Polish the piece. This kind of work looks better when the high points are well polished, providing a contrast to those areas that have been scorched by the flame.

MAKING EASY SOLDER

1 If all goes horribly wrong the resulting mess can be mixed with copper or brass to make solder. For easy solder use two parts silver to one part brass, and for hard solder, three parts silver to one part copper. Ball up both metals (see page 90) and allow them to mix.

2 When the bead of metal begins to spin, this is an indication that it is completely molten. When it has cooled, soak it well in the acid pickle.

3 Flatten the bead on a steel plate using a hammer, and remove any spent flux or remaining bits of firebrick with coarse emery paper. Roll out the bead into a thin sheet about 1/64 in (0.3 mm) thick using a rolling mill. Anneal the solder part of the way through this process to avoid cracks appearing at the edges.

REPOUSSÉ

Repoussé is the process of creating relief designs from flat sheet metal using punches. The work is carried out from the back as well as from the front of the design. You need to use a yielding surface that will allow the metal to sink where the punch strikes, but which will also support the surrounding metal. This surface is traditionally made of pitch mixed with varying ratios of plaster, to stiffen the mixture, and beeswax, to soften it. The punches required for repoussé are all different shapes and sizes. A good collection of repoussé punches can run to twenty or thirty, but a start can be made with seven or eight.

LESSON: REPOUSSÉ TECHNIQUES

Work in repoussé usually consists of three stages—tracing or lining in, blocking, and matting. Tracing is the process of creating the design outline on the front of the metal using thin punches. Blocking involves turning the work over and working on it from the reverse with larger and more rounded punches. Matting is the creation of a pattern or texture on the work, usually as a background to the main design. Planishing punches are sometimes used on the front of the work to smooth off the finished surface.

YOU WILL NEED
- Pitch mixture
- Hemispherical iron bowl
- Ring of wood, leather, or rope
- Soldering torch
- Paraffin
- Wood block
- Broad-headed carpet tacks
- Handsaw
- A selection of repoussé punches including tracing, blocking, matting, and planishing punches

USING PITCH

The preferred container for the pitch mixture is a hemispherical iron bowl resting on a ring of wood, leather, or rope. This allows the surface of the pitch to be tilted, but any container of wood or metal will do. Pitch can be bought from specialist jewelry suppliers in a block, which is then broken up and melted into the container. You must repeatedly melt the pitch with a soldering torch and clean the work with paraffin.

USING A WOOD BLOCK

If the kitchen table is your workplace you may find that a block of wood is a more suitable alternative to a pitch bowl. To begin the repoussé projects in this section you will need a wood block about 4¾ in (120 mm) square. The wood must have a uniform grain—sycamore or maple is ideal, but most softwoods are suitable. Any wood with pronounced rings, such as oak or pitch pine, is not suitable. Use the end grain for repoussé, and the sides for drilling on or for matting. Hold the work down with broad-headed carpet tacks. As the surface of the wood becomes compressed, face it off with a handsaw.

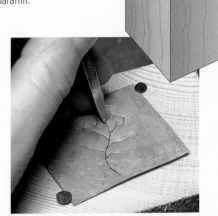

DESIGNING IN REPOUSSÉ

Repoussé is a versatile technique which can be used to create the most complex and intricate designs. With long practice you can use repoussé to make accurate images of natural forms such as fish, birds, and animals. As an introduction to the technique of repoussé, designs based on simple circles, arcs, and curves are most accessible. These basic elements, which can be shaped using templates and specialist punches, can be developed into quite complex designs reminiscent of some Celtic examples. Leaf designs are relatively easy to create with repoussé, and, being fairly flat, are better suited to a wood block

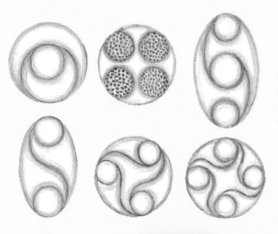

Geometric shapes are the easiest to achieve in repoussé.

Repoussé can be used to create beautiful and highly intricate designs like this.

MODELING

Repoussé can be a time-consuming technique, so before beginning a project it is a good idea to make a model to test your design. The aluminum used to make beer cans makes good modeling material, as does the foil around the neck of some wine bottles. You can use a dry ballpoint pen as your tracing tool and a teaspoon handle or the end of a fountain pen for a blocking tool. A telephone directory or a couple of newspapers are ideal substitutes for a pitch bed.

REPOUSSÉ PUNCHES

All repoussé punches have slightly rounded edges to prevent digging into the metal. They are also highly polished except for the matting punches, which must retain their definition of texture.

The pitch bowl is an iron hemisphere that is usually supported on a ring.

PROJECT 30 BRONZE REPOUSSÉ RING

YOU WILL NEED

- Bench peg
- Annealing equipment (see page 30)
- 2¾ x ²⁵⁄₆₄ x ¹⁄₆₄ in (66 x 10 x 0.5 mm) bronze strip
- Pencil
- Wood block
- Carpet tacks
- ⁵⁄₁₆ in (8 mm) and ¹⁵⁄₆₄ (6 mm) circle punches
- ⁵⁄₁₆ in (8 mm) and ¹⁵⁄₆₄ (6 mm) ball bearings
- Hammer
- Matting punch
- Jeweler's shears
- File
- Emery board
- Soldering equipment (see page 31)
- 2¾ x ²⁵⁄₆₄ x ¹⁄₆₄ in (68 x 10 x 0.5 mm) silver strip
- Tapered mandrel
- 45° beveled punch
- Vise
- Polishing equipment (see page 34)

This simple bronze ring makes an ideal introduction to repoussé. The silver lining prevents staining of the skin and also increases the overall thickness of the ring.

1 Anneal the bronze, then mark out the centers of what will be about eight domes with a pencil. Draw guidelines down each side. The domes are ²³⁄₆₄ in (9 mm) apart. Secure the bronze strip down to the end grain of a wood block with carpet tacks. Punch the circles, alternating between a ⁵⁄₁₆ in (8 mm) and ¹⁵⁄₆₄ in (6 mm) circle punch.

Cross-section of punch showing center-drilled hole.

Circle punches.

2 Turn the work over and, resting a ball bearing in each of the little circular hollows, give it a sharp tap with a hammer in order to raise the dome.

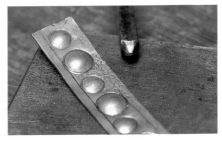

3 Now work on the metal from the front again. Using a matting punch, cover the metal around the domes with punch marks. You can do this on the side of the wood block or on a flat piece of steel.

4 File the ends of the bronze strip square on the bench peg and solder the strip into a ring. Make the ring round using a mallet on a tapered mandrel. Use a 1 in (25 mm) 45° beveled punch to open out both sides of the bronze ring. Line the bronze ring with a thin strip of silver (see Steps 7–8, page 93). Insert the silver ring into the bronze one and punch it as for the bronze one to make it captive.

PROJECT 31 REPOUSSÉ PENDANT

| TECHNIQUES COVERED • Annealing • Repoussé • Drilling • Cutting • Polishing |

The silver ring around this bronze pendant serves as a frame as well as a hanging device.
The circular domes and their connecting grooves are reminiscent of much Celtic design.

YOU WILL NEED

- 2 x 2 x ½ in (50 x 50 x 0.7 mm) bronze sheet
- Iron binding wire
- Clear adhesive tape
- Hammer
- Wood block
- Carpet tacks
- ²⁵⁄₆₄ in (10 mm) steel rod
- Pair of compasses
- ⁵⁄₁₆ in (8 mm) circle punch
- Lining punch
- Blocking punch
- Dividers
- Center punch
- Cross-punch (see page 14)
- Electric drill and ¹⁄₁₆ in (1.5 mm) bit
- Jeweler's shears
- Emery boards of varying grades
- Burnisher
- Polishing equipment (see page 34)
- 4¾ x ⁵⁄₆₄ in (120 x 2 mm) round silver wire
- Soldering equipment (see page 31)
- Round former
- Four silver jump rings
- Two parallel-jawed pliers

1 Tracing the outline of your design with a lining punch is often the most difficult stage of repoussé. To make it easier, make a ring of iron binding wire, 1 in (25 mm) in diameter, and fix it to the bronze sheet with clear adhesive tape. Fasten the metal sheet to the end grain of the wood block with carpet tacks.

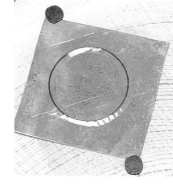

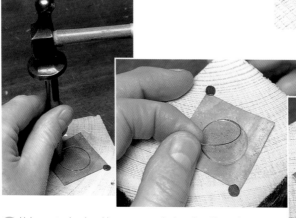

2 Using a steel rod and hammer, punch the wire all round to create an indent. Remove the wire, then with a pair of compasses set to the radius of the circle, mark three equidistant points on the circumference.

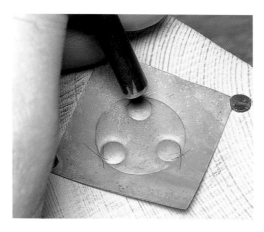

3 With the three points on the circumference as your guide, use a ⁵⁄₁₆ in (8 mm) circle punch to create three circles within the large circle. You will find it easy to feel the punch into place.

4 Create three S-shaped lines using the same wire-and-punch technique as for the outer circle. With all the lines established, go over the design with a lining punch and hammer. Lean the punch away from you and work along the line toward you, resting your little finger on the metal. The punch should move along its path a little way with each hammer blow. You will need to move the work continually to allow the punch to remain at the same angle.

Leaning the punch away from you will enable you to see its path more clearly.

5 Turn the work over to block it in from the reverse. To do this, gently hammer a blocking punch into the areas between the lines of the design. Hold the punch in an upright position, resting it lightly on the surface. When moving the punch continually over the metal, try to merge the punch marks into each other with rapid hammer blows. This creates a relief effect on the front of the metal.

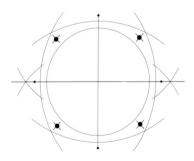

This diagram illustrates the pendant outline and the position of the four holes near the points where the arcs cross.

6 Turn the work again and retrace the lines of the design with the lining punch. To mark out the four sides of the finished piece that surround the circle, strike a cross through the circle center and mark four points, ⅛ in (3 mm) outside the circle, at north, south, east, and west points. Center punch each point then, placing one point of the dividers at each of these points, scribe four arcs 5⁄64 in (2 mm) away from the circle. Center punch four hole positions near the four points where the arcs cross.

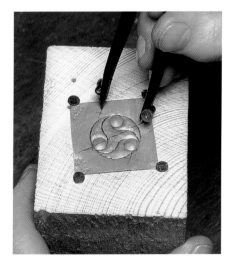

7 Using a cross-punch, matt in the background. Reinforce the center-punched hole positions. Drill the four holes to 1/16 in (1.5 mm) in diameter.

8 Cut out the shape with jeweler's shears. Finish the edges with emery boards, a burnisher, and polishing pads.

9 To make the silver hanging ring that surrounds the circle, file the ends of the round silver wire square and bend the wire into shape. Solder the join and file off any surplus solder. Make the ring round on a former such as the neck of a wine bottle.

10 Insert four silver jump rings into each of the four holes on the edges of the pendant, opening each one slightly using two parallel-jawed pliers (see page 121). Insert the silver wire into the jump rings. The hanging ring and jump rings must be the correct size for the frame to fit into place correctly (see right).

WORKING IN ACRYLIC

Acrylic has been used by jewelry makers ever since it became widely available. Of all the non-metal materials it is perhaps the most useful. Most often used in sheet form, acrylic comes in a wide range of bright colors, as opaque or translucent and also clear. Being light in weight it can be used in large pieces; even earrings can be quite chunky when made of acrylic. Acrylic is a tactile material, inviting to the touch, and its optical properties are superior to glass. Acrylic can be sawn with a hacksaw or a coping saw. It can be drilled, filed, abraded, and highly polished, using similar techniques to those used on metal. Adhesives are available for acrylic, but these sometimes present problems in use and may degrade over the long term. Acrylic is not resistant to scratching, but scratches are easily removed. Acrylic softens, and becomes plastic at about 338°F (170°C). At this temperature you can handle it comfortably with gloved hands, and you can bend, mold, and even weld it using moderate sustained pressure. This low softening temperature can be a problem, however, and the friction from sawing, abrading, or polishing too vigorously can soften the surface of acrylic with unhappy results.

ABRADING ACRYLIC

A plentiful supply of emery paper is invaluable when you are working with acrylic. Emery papers are most useful when stuck down to boards with double-sided adhesive tape. A disc sanding machine is particularly useful, and the one shown here is homemade using the motor from an old washing machine.

SAWING ACRYLIC

A bandsaw will make light work of slicing blocks of acrylic, but a coarse hacksaw blade will do the same job given time.

This arrangement of a hacksaw blade screwed down to a board with spacers can be used as a substitute for a bandsaw.

LESSON: LAMINATING ACRYLIC

Laminating acrylic presents exciting possibilities to the jewelry maker. When finished to a high polish the brightly colored, banded material looks striking, particularly when set in silver. Translucent or tinted colors are very effective in this process, more so when combined with clear sheets. The satisfaction of watching the rough sawn block being transformed into a brilliant jewel is unsurpassed in any area of jewelry making.

YOU WILL NEED

- Two 4 x 2 x ²⁵⁄₆₄ in (100 x 50 x 10 mm) mild steel plates
- Two hexagonal or square-headed bolts
- 2¹¹⁄₆₄ x 1⁴⁹⁄₆₄ x 1¼ in (55 x 45 x 5 mm) acrylic sheets
- Soapy water
- Oven
- Spanner
- Gloves
- Parallel-jawed pliers
- Vise
- Bandsaw or hacksaw with coarse blade
- Simple jig
- Coping saw
- Rasps
- Coarse files
- Emery boards
- Disc sander

POINTS TO NOTE

- Overheating or heating for too long will cause bubbles to appear in the work. If you spot these in time they will only be near the surface of the material and will be squeezed out to the sides and trimmed off as waste. Undercooking can result in some of the layers coming apart, and occasionally, splitting apart at the squeezing stage.

1 The simple press is made from mild steel plates measuring 4 x 2 x ²⁵⁄₆₄ in (100 x 50 x 10 mm) with holes at either end. The plates are held together by hexagonal or square-headed bolts. Make sure the acrylic sheets are clean and free from dust before starting the process; this is best achieved by washing them in soapy water. In this size of press the pieces must be 2¹¹⁄₆₄ x 1⁴⁹⁄₆₄ in (55 x 45 mm). Sandwich contrasting layers of acrylic to a depth of about 1⅜ in (35 mm) between the plates. Place in the center of a pre-heated oven at about 338°F (170°C) for about an hour.

3 After being allowed to cool, saw the laminated acrylic into slices. For the best effect make the initial cut diagonally. This is most easily done with a bandsaw, or alternatively with a hacksaw fitted with a coarse blade. Once you have made the first cut, you can make slices using a simple jig.

2 When the acrylic has softened, wear gloves to remove the clamp from the oven with parallel-jawed pliers. Fasten it securely in a vise. Tighten the nuts until the sandwich is reduced in thickness by about 40 percent, or is approximately ²⁵⁄₃₂ in (20 mm) thick. To be successful this process requires that the heat should penetrate right into the core of the material, making it plastic throughout.

4 Cut the sliced sections with a coping saw and shape them with rasps, coarse files, and emery boards. The most effective method of rough shaping is with a disc sander (see page 104).

YOU WILL NEED

- 2 x 1³⁷⁄₆₄ x ¹³⁄₆₄ in (50 x 40 x 5 mm) unlaminated acrylic
- Permanent marker pen
- Toggle clamp
- Smooth plywood
- Drill and ¹⁵⁄₆₄ and ⁵⁄₃₂ in (6 and 4 mm) bits
- Countersink
- Vise
- Two blocks of wood
- Hacksaw
- Abrasive boards
- Polishing equipment (see page 34)

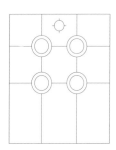

PROJECT 32 ACRYLIC CROSS

TECHNIQUES COVERED ● Drilling ● Polishing

This acrylic cross relies for its effect on its highly polished edges, including the countersinks, and on the subtle tone and clarity of the material.

1 Mark out the positions of five holes (see picture below) on the protective film. Place the acrylic on a smooth piece of plywood, clamp it securely with the toggle clamp and drill the holes. Countersink the four large holes on the back and front.

POINTS TO NOTE

- When drilling acrylic, always have a smooth piece of plywood under it. This prevents fragments breaking off when the drill comes through the bottom of the hole. Never force or jerk the drill as this can cause the material to crack.

2 Hold the acrylic in a vise using two blocks of wood as vise guards. Saw down each line with a hacksaw, taking care not to follow through with the saw as you break into the holes.

3 Smooth all the edges, starting with coarse, then medium, and fine abrasive. Finally, polish the edges on a polishing machine or on a pad.

4 Finally, only after all the finishing has been carried out, peel off the protective film.

YOU WILL NEED

- Piece of laminated acrylic (see page 105)
- Plywood
- Double-sided adhesive tape
- Hacksaw
- Disc sander
- Emery boards
- Electric drill and 1/16 in (1.5 mm) drill bit
- 4 x 1/2 in (100 x 1 mm) round silver wire
- Balling up equipment (see page 90)
- End cutters
- Parallel-jawed pliers
- End cutters
- Two ear wires

PROJECT 33 ACRYLIC EARRINGS

TECHNIQUES COVERED ● Drilling ● Balling Up

These simple faceted earrings show off the translucent red and gray acrylic to very good effect. As the viewing angle changes the appearance is transformed.

1 Stick the laminated acrylic to a plywood base with double-sided adhesive tape and saw it in half to create the basic tapered form.

2 Create the facets (the flat faces between the sharp points on the earrings) using a disc sander. There are no hard and fast rules to this process, but you may find it easier to decide on the position of each facet if you smooth them down on an emery board as you proceed. Working on each stage of both earrings together will help you to make them as near identical as possible.

3 File a little flat area to give the drill a starting place, then, over a plywood base, drill the hole.

  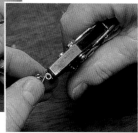

SAFETY CONSIDERATIONS

● Like all fine dust, the dust from acrylic can be harmful, so it is recommended that you wear a mask. Be sure to sweep up any acrylic dust; if it builds up on floor surfaces it can make them slippery. When using a disc sander, never apply heavy pressure as this will cause the build-up of heat with harmful consequences. A vacuum cleaner makes an effective dust extractor; simply drill a hole in the side of your machine to accommodate the hose.

4 To make the hanging device, ball up the end of a piece of round silver wire and cut off 1 3/16 in (30 mm), including the ball. File a taper on the other end. Push the wire through the hole in the acrylic with the ball at the front. Bend the wire using parallel-jawed pliers with one jaw resting on the ball. Bend the wire to point to the front then scroll up the tapered end to form a ring which can be connected to the ear wire.

PROJECT 34 ACRYLIC CABOCHON

TECHNIQUES COVERED ● Polishing ● Abrading

YOU WILL NEED
- Piece of laminated acrylic
- Card template
- ¹⁹⁄₃₂ in (15 mm) plywood
- Permanent marker pen
- Coping saw
- Vise
- Disc sander
- Wooden guides
- Double-sided adhesive tape
- Coarse to medium emery boards
- Fine emery papers
- Acrylic polishing compound
- Sanding machine
- Polishing equipment (see page 34)
- Penknife

This distinctively shaped cabochon works equally well as a pendant as for a choker. The rich colors of the acrylic are combined to good effect, particularly when mounted in silver.

1 Mark the outline of the cabochon onto the piece of laminated acrylic using a card template of the shape below and a permanent pen. Try to choose the most promising section of the material.

The cabochon shape.

2 Cut out the shape in the acrylic with a coping saw. This is most easily done with the work held in a vise. Finish to the line on a disc sander.

3 Saw out a piece of plywood or MDF, using the template to mark out the shape, and stick the acrylic work onto it with double-sided adhesive tape. You will need to apply firm pressure to make a secure bond. This will make the work easier to hold and will protect your knuckles from the abrasives.

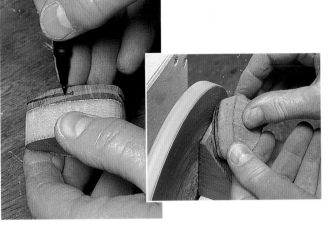

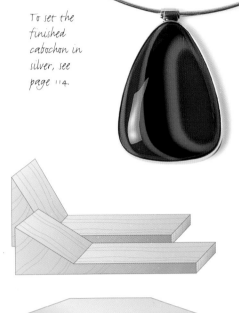

To set the finished cabochon in silver, see page 114.

4 Mark a guideline around the work with the permanent pen, then bevel the edge on the disc sander. This is made easier if you use guides that support the work against the sanding disc at the correct angle.

Rest the acrylic against the guides (right) for support. At this stage the beveled piece should look like the shape right (below) when seen in profile.

5 Bring the work to a fully rounded shape using coarse to medium emery boards. Hold the work loosely in the hand and wipe it over the emery board, rocking it as you do so, turning it slightly with each stroke. This will remove the corners and the flat area in the center.

6 Bring the surface to a smooth finish using finer emery papers. At this stage it will be easier to achieve a rounded form with loose paper held in your fingers. Faults will become apparent on the smoother surface, and you will need to return to coarser abrasives to remove them.

7 Polishing, using acrylic polishing compound, will also expose tiny imperfections which will necessitate recourse to rough measures. There is no alternative to this procedure. To finish off the edges and reverse of the cabochon, remove the acrylic cabochon from the plywood by sliding a penknife under it and gently levering it off.

SETTING STONES

Semi-precious stones are most commonly found in the form of cabochons. These are smooth, domed shapes with a flat back, usually oval or round. The contour varies from hemispherical to more or less flat. The method of setting relies on the fact that all cabochons are widest at their base.

YOU WILL NEED

- ⅝ in (8 mm) round cabochon
- Dividers
- 1 x ¹⁄₆₄ in (25 x 0.3 mm) strip of bezel silver
- Jeweler's shears
- Soldering equipment (see page 31)
- Tapered mandrel
- Planishing hammer
- Rolled-hide mallet
- Emery board
- 2 x 1³⁄₁₆ x ½ in (50 x 30 x 0.8 mm) bronze strip
- Penknife
- Adhesive tape
- Pusher
- Burnisher

LESSON: **BEZEL SETTING**

The outline shape of this bronze pendant does not matter; just make it any shape you like.

The only requirement is that the surface should be evenly dished to allow the round bezel to fit.

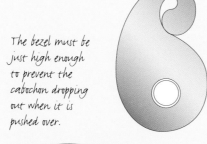

The bezel must be just high enough to prevent the cabochon dropping out when it is pushed over.

1 Measure the edge of the cabochon with dividers to determine the height of the bezel. The contours of cabochons vary; there must be enough height to secure the stone, but not so much as will obscure too much of it. Err on the side of too wide to allow for finishing.

2 With the dividers set at this width, scribe a line on the bezel silver, then cut off the narrow strip. Bend it to shape with your fingers and join the ends using hard solder.

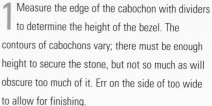

3 Make the bezel round on a tapered mandrel, then planish it until it stretches to slide down onto the untapered section. Check that your cabochon passes freely through the bezel, then rub it on an emery board to make it flat and clean.

4 Clean the bronze strip—the area that is to receive the bezel—by placing it in acid pickle. Place the bronze strip on a tripod. Dip the bezel in the flux; then, holding it with tweezers, place it in position on the bronze strip. When you remove it a light ring of flux will be left behind. Carefully place four pallions of easy solder around the ring, then balance the bezel over the pallions.

5 Solder the bezel into place on the bronze by heating the work from beneath the tripod. For a moment the bezel will remain black, then, as the solder melts, the heat will quickly transfer to the thin silver, which will settle obligingly into place.

6 When setting translucent stones like the carnelian used here you must first scrape the metal within the bezel setting so that the stone appears clean and bright. Use the small blade of a penknife to do this. Use the same tool to scrape off any burrs on the inside of the bezel.

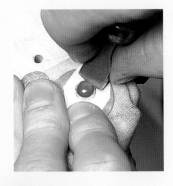

7 Protect the area around the bezel with adhesive tape to prevent accidental damage from the pusher or burnisher. Then, with the stone in position, push the top edge of the bezel onto the stone with the pusher. Work on the edge of the bezel, pressing down at four points that are roughly at 90 degrees to each other, before pressing between these points until there are no gaps between bezel and stone.

The pusher must press on the top edge of the bezel.

8 With the stone firmly set in place, use a burnisher to smooth and polish the edge of the bezel. Hold the burnisher tightly and use your thumb to prevent the point of the tool touching the surface of the surrounding metal.

The burnisher imparts a bright polish to the metal lying next to the stone.

YOU WILL NEED

- 2³⁄₁₆ x ⁵⁄₁₆ x ¹⁄₃₂ in (70 x 8 x 0.8 mm) silver ring
- Annealing equipment (see page 30)
- Doming block
- Small block of hardwood or steel
- Heavy hammer
- ¹⁵⁄₆₄ in (6 mm) cabochon
- Bezel setting equipment (see page 110)
- ¾ x ¹⁄₁₂₈ in (19 x 0.25 mm) strip of bezel silver
- Steel rod
- Bezel setting equipment (see page 110)
- Ring clamp
- Polishing equipment (see page 34)

PROJECT 35 DOMED RING WITH CABOCHON

TECHNIQUES COVERED ● Annealing ● Bezel Setting ● Polishing

Mounting a stone on a ring can be difficult as the bezel must be shaped to fit the curve of the ring. These two ring projects offer different solutions to this problem.

1 Anneal a silver ring. Place the ring edge-on into a doming block; use the smallest dome into which it will fit. Place a block of hardwood or metal on the ring and hammer it until the ring begins to turn inward. Turn it over and punch it from the other side, keeping the block square to the work.

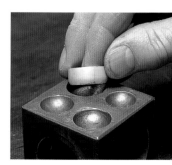

A lot of force is required for this process so use a heavy hammer.

2 With the ring domed, make a ¹⁵⁄₆₄ in (6 mm) bezel, which, when you have made it flat on the emery board, should fit your domed ring. Solder this into position, placing the pallions on the inside, leaning against the bezel. Support the ring with a steel rod bent at right angles when soldering the setting in place.

3 Hold the ring in a ring clamp. This will make it easier to push the bezel onto the cabochon. Finishing is made easier by the fact that the metal surrounding the setting slopes away in all directions.

POINTS TO NOTE

● The thickness of bezel material is a compromise. If it is too thin, joining is more difficult, and the risk of melting is increased. If a bezel is too thick it can be difficult to push it against the stone, particularly on smaller stones.

YOU WILL NEED

- 2 ⁹⁄₁₆ x ²⁵⁄₆₄ x ¹⁄₃₂ in (65 x 10 x 0.8 mm) strip of silver
- Bezel setting equipment (see page 110)
- ²⁵⁄₃₂ x ²⁵⁄₆₄ x ¹⁄₃₂ in (20 x 10 x 0.8 mm) silver strip
- Piercing saw
- 1 x ¹⁄₆₄ in (25 x 0.3 mm) strip of bezel silver
- Hand file
- ⁵⁄₁₆ in (8 mm) tapered mandrel
- ⁵⁄₁₆ in (8 mm) cabochon
- Ring clamp
- Polishing equipment (see page 34)

PROJECT 36 PLATFORM RING WITH CABOCHON

TECHNIQUES COVERED ● Forming ● Soldering ● Cutting ● Bezel Setting ● Polishing

In this ring a platform is soldered to the ring metal, providing a flat surface for the bezel to rest on. It is essential to file the two pieces so that they are flat and smooth over the area where they meet, to ensure that soldering is successful.

Rub the two mating surfaces on an emery board to ensure that both are flat and clean.

1 Form the 2 ⁹⁄₁₆ in (65 mm) silver strip into a ring, but when shaping, make the flat section either side of the join longer than usual. For the platform, saw and file the ends of the smaller piece of silver to shape. File both elements with emery boards where they will meet. Solder the piece to the ring blank while both are still flat.

2 Using a mallet and planishing hammer where necessary, form the ring to shape on the tapered mandrel. Then file the area of the platform metal that is to receive the bezel until flat.

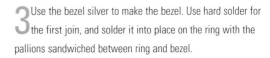

3 Use the bezel silver to make the bezel. Use hard solder for the first join, and solder it into place on the ring with the pallions sandwiched between ring and bezel.

4 You may wish to taper the back of this ring. Use a piercing saw to cut it roughly to shape then finish it on an emery board. The cabochon is set in the same way as for the domed ring (see page 112).

LESSON: SETTING LARGE AND ODD-SHAPED CABOCHONS

YOU WILL NEED

- Acrylic cabochon (see page 108)
- Adhesive tape
- Scissors
- Length of ¹³⁄₆₄ in (5 mm) silver bearer wire
- Soldering equipment (see page 31)
- Strip bending pliers (see page 16)
- 1³⁄₁₆ x ¹⁵⁄₆₄ x ¹⁄₆₄ in (30 x 6 x 0.3 mm) silver strip
- Annealing equipment (see page 30)
- Planishing hammer

The mounting of a large, unusually shaped cabochon presents its own problems. Here the acrylic cabochon made on page 108 is set in silver.

1 Cabochons of this size are normally set with an open back using commercially made bearer wire. To calculate the perimeter of an odd shape, take a narrow length of adhesive tape and wrap it around the edge of the cabochon, then make a cut where the tape overlaps. This will give you the perimeter of the cabochon, but you need to add a small amount to allow for the thickness of the bearer wire.

2 Solder the bearer wire into a ring, placing the pallions on the outside to make it easier to clean off any surplus solder.

3 Bend the setting into the shape of the cabochon using first your fingers and then strip bending pliers. The join should be at the bottom away from where the hanging device is to be attached.

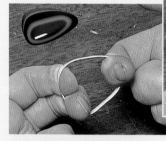

4 Make the hanging device by cutting a taper on the 1³⁄₁₆ in (30 mm) length of silver to ¹⁄₃₂ in (1 mm), leaving ²⁵⁄₆₄ in (10 mm) of metal at full width. Anneal the silver and roll it up, starting at the broad end until about ⅛ in (3 mm) of flat metal remains. Flood solder onto the base and on the front of the roll.

5 Solder the little roll into place by placing the bezel on top of the straight section and against the roll. Flux well, place small pallions between the roll and bezel, and reheat from the inside.

Tapered silver.

Roll up and solder with pallions.

YOU WILL NEED

- 1³⁄₆₄ x ¹⁄₁₆ x ¹⁄₆₄ in (29 x 2 x 0.3 mm) strip of bezel silver
- ²⁵⁄₆₄ x ⁵⁄₁₆ in (10 x 8 mm) oval cabochon
- Fork or spoon handle in silver or nickel silver
- Hand file
- Cabochon setting equipment (see page 114)
- End cutters

PROJECT 37 FORK HANDLE PENDANT

TECHNIQUES COVERED ● Bezel Setting ● Soldering ● Annealing

Round cabochons are generally easier to mount, but on a fairly flat object an oval stone presents few problems. This pendant is made from an old silver fork.

1 Form the bezel strip into a ring, and join the ends with hard solder. Press the bezel between your finger and thumb to make it oval—the join should be on one of the long sides. Check that the cabochon passes through freely. If not, return the bezel to the mandrel and planish it lightly to stretch it.

2 Snip off the handle using end cutters—how much of the shank you allow for the making of the hook depends on the design of the handle. In this case there is a little over 1³⁄₁₆ in (30 mm) above the design. File down the front of the shank to a gradual taper, and file the end into a blunt point.

3 Solder the bezel into place on the fork handle, resting it on six easy solder pallions and heating from beneath.

4 Set the cabochon into the bezel. Polish the work before bending the end backward away from the face, then over to form the hook. Make sure the end is annealed.

CASTING IN PEWTER

There is no more dramatic way of transforming metal than by casting. The pouring of molten metal is always exciting, and then there is usually a tense wait while the mold cools to reveal success—or failure. Casting may well have been the first process used by the earliest metalworker, when he hollowed out an ax-head shape in a rock and poured molten copper alloy into it. Whenever you see a complex solid form with realistic detail created in silver, it has probably been cast in a mold.

Casting metal is one of the most delicate processes in jewelry making and the melting of silver requires high temperatures and specialized equipment. An alternative metal that affords a safer and easier introduction to casting is pewter. Of course pewter is no substitute for silver but it has the great benefits of being inexpensive and easy to melt. Using it will provide you with an appreciation of the immense potential of the casting process.

Pewter melts at about 572°F (300°C), compared to silver, which melts at 1640°F (893°C). So you can melt pewter on a kitchen stove in a kitchen ladle. You can even make your molds out of wood as the metal will cool before the wood has had time to burn.

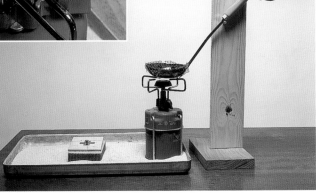

A camping stove has been used as a heat source for the projects in this book, but you could also use a kitchen stove or soldering torch. You may find the wooden stand shown here useful, too—it is easily made using two woodscrews to support the ladle at the correct height. A tray of sand will catch any spillage from the melting process.

LESSON: PEWTER PENDANT

An open mold is used for this pendant cross, which creates a soft, rounded form. The woodscrew creates a hole by which the pendant is hung.

YOU WILL NEED

- Piece of plywood
- Piercing saw
- Nails and hammer
- Block of grainy wood
- Woodscrew
- Screwdriver and electric drill
- Soft pencil
- Tray of sand
- Camping stove
- Metal ladle with wire mesh covering
- Pewter

1 Begin by sawing out a shape in the center of the plywood with a piercing saw. Nail the mold to the wood block into which you have screwed the woodscrew. Position the mold carefully to leave the woodscrew in the correct position for the pendant hole and pinch the entry saw-cut closed as you nail it down. If you rub all around the woodscrew with a soft pencil this will make it easier to remove when the time comes.

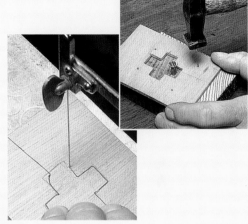

2 Melt a small amount of pewter in the ladle and pour it into the open mold. The wire mesh covering the front of the ladle will sieve any impurities out. Rock the mold gently to ensure that the metal reaches into all the corners.

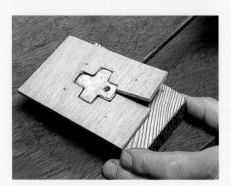

3 Remove the woodscrew before prising off the plywood to release the pendant. If you are not completely happy with the result, you may repeat the process several times using the same metal and mold.

PROJECT 38 PEWTER KEY RING

YOU WILL NEED

- A block of grainy wood 4 x 3 x 25⁄64 in (100 x 75 x 60 mm)
- Penknife
- Strips of 3⁄4 x 1⁄8 x in (20 x 3 mm) plywood
- Soldering torch
- Brass brush
- Piercing saw
- Hammer
- Small panel pins
- G clamps
- Camping stove
- Ladle
- Pewter

TECHNIQUES COVERED ● Cutting ● Casting

This project makes use of a closed, or two-part mold which gives a sharp impression of the wood grain.

1 Use a saw to slice the wood block into two pieces 1 13⁄64 in (30 mm) thick. Carve a little "V" on the top edge of both pieces to act as a sprue. Scorch the inside of both pieces with a soldering torch then rub them with a brass brush. This will enhance the impression of the wood grain and also dry up any moisture in the wood.

2 Now cut out some little triangles from the plywood with a piercing saw, and pin them to one side of your mold. Complete this side of the mold with two little pieces at the top to form the pouring hole.

3 Clamp the two halves of the mold together using two or more G clamps. It is important that the two sides fit closely together with no gaps, except for the tiny gaps created by the wood grain, through which air will be allowed to escape.

SAFETY CONSIDERATIONS

- Pewter used to be made up of about 20 percent lead, which is highly toxic. Do not be tempted to melt down old teapots and tankards. Only use lead-free pewter. Seek advice from your supplier who will advise you of the most suitable alloy for your purposes.

4 Now melt the pewter in the ladle and pour it into the mold. Be sure to pour it in one continuous stream.

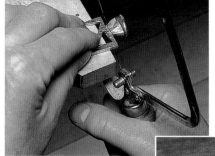

5 Leave the pewter for five or ten minutes until you are sure that the casting has cooled. Take off the clamps and open the mold. Prise off the plywood strips all round before you release the casting. Do this carefully as soft pewter is easily damaged.

POINTS TO NOTE

- Molten metal can be dangerous so always use googles and gloves when pouring it.
- Hot metal looks the same as cold metal so handle with care until you know it be cold.
- Always use dry wood; if in doubt, scorch it with the soldering torch.
- Try out different patterns of wood grain—use the end grain as well as the side.

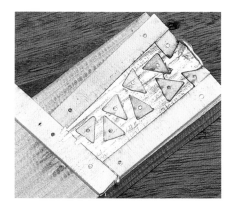

6 Saw off the sprue with a piercing saw, then give the finished piece a thorough brushing with a brass brush to bring out the distinctive sheen.

CHAINS AND CATCHES

Long ago, when a jeweler needed a catch, a link, or a pin, he would search around in the scraps on his bench and "find" a suitable piece of metal with which to make it. So the name "findings" came to be used for all those small components used to connect or fasten the earrings, bracelets, and necklaces made by the jeweler. There is a finding to satisfy the jewelry maker's every need. It would be foolish to try to make those items that can be bought very cheaply, but there are projects where the catch or chain can be a distinctive piece of jewelry and an end in itself.

store-bought findings.

LESSON: FETTER CHAIN

This style of chain is called a fetter chain. The long link makes it easy to build up a substantial length of chain quite quickly. Here it is used as a bracelet but of course with added links it could be a necklace or even a belt.

YOU WILL NEED
- 20 x ³⁄₆₄ in (500 x 1.2 mm) round silver wire
- ⅛ in (3 mm) dowel
- Smooth-jawed vise
- Adhesive tape
- Piercing saw
- Soldering equipment (see page 31)
- Round-nosed pliers
- Parallel-jawed pliers
- Planishing hammer and stake
- Hand file

JUMP RINGS

1 Begin by making jump rings. Cut off 6 in (150 mm) of wire and wrap it tightly around the end of the dowel.

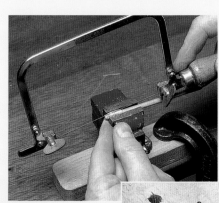

2 Hold the coil in the vise and saw down the whole coil with a piercing saw. Use the finest saw blade you have as this will be least likely to snag. If you don't have a suitable vise you can hold the dowel against a bench peg while you saw. Wrap adhesive tape around the coil to keep the rings tidy until you have completed the saw cut. You should always make more than your immediate requirements, as you will always need jump rings for jewelry work.

FETTER LINKS

3 Now make the fetter links. Cut the rest of the wire into 1⅜ in (36 mm) lengths and solder them into rings. Pull them into an elongated shape using round-nosed pliers. Use the parallel-jawed pliers to make the sides straight. Planish the links at this stage, including the jump rings, and give them a polish. The jump rings can be threaded on to the dowel for polishing.

4 Assemble the chain by joining pairs of fetter links with jump rings. Then join the pairs together to make fours and the fours to make eight, and so on.

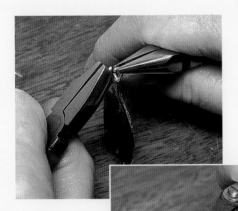

5 Jump rings should be opened sideways with a shearing action, rather than being pulled apart. In this way the rounded shape of the ring is preserved. Use two pairs of pliers if you have them, if not make yourself a holding device from a file handle and a slotted head wood screw.

Never pull jump rings apart as this will lead to distortion.

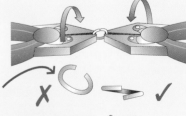

✗ Incorrect.   Correct. ✓

LESSON: T-BAR TOGGLE CATCH

*The "T" bar was originally used to fasten the ends of watch chains into button holes. With
a ring it makes a suitable fastening for a bracelet as it is easy to fasten with one hand.*

YOU WILL NEED
- Fetter link and jump rings (see page 120)
- ¹⁄₁₆ in (1.5 mm) steel rod
- Bench peg
- Soldering equipment (see page 31)
- 4 x ⁵⁄₆₄ in (100 x 2 mm) round silver wire
- Parallel-jawed pliers
- Tapered punch
- Planishing hammer and stake
- Ring mandrel

1 Take a single fetter link and squeeze the sides together around the steel rod fixed in the bench peg until the sides meet. Solder the sides together using hard solder to leave a little closed ring at either end.

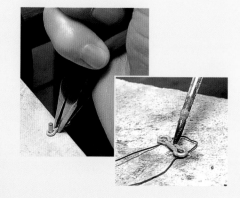

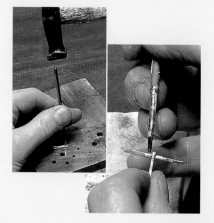

2 Open the end rings with the tapered punch over a hole until both are round and one of them is a tight fit around the ⁵⁄₆₄ in (2 mm) silver wire. Cut off 1³⁄₁₆ in (30 mm) of this wire and solder it into the hole using a large pallion of easy solder at either side. Make sure the two ends are the same length, then file the ends flat and polish.

3 Make a ring from 2¹¹⁄₆₄ x ⁵⁄₆₄ in (55 x 2 mm) round silver wire. Solder into a ring and make it round on a mandrel. With parallel-jawed pliers, squeeze the two opposing sides to create a flat, making a kind of running track shape.

4 Planish the face and edges and polish well. If you bend the ring slightly at this stage this will make for a better fit around the "T" bar created in Steps 1–2. Now join each part to the ends of the fetter chain with jump rings. A slightly larger ring will be needed to accommodate the thicker wire of the ring. For this catch to be secure the "T" bar should only just fit between the ring down its length.

PROJECT 39 BEADS BRACELET

YOU WILL NEED

- 40 x ³⁄₆₄ in (1000 x 1.3 mm) round silver wire
- File
- Planishing hammer and flat stake
- Piercing saw
- End cutters
- Round-nosed pliers
- Parallel-jawed pliers
- Ten ⁵⁄₁₆ in (8 mm) beads
- Polishing equipment (see page 34)
- Bolt ring
- ⅛ in (3 mm) dowel

TECHNIQUES COVERED ● Planishing ● Soldering ● Polishing

Beads were probably the earliest form of jewelry and this is not surprising as most people would find it easy to thread a bead onto a thread. When beads are combined with silver the two complement each other and here they are used to make an effective chain.

1 Cut the silver wire into ten 3³⁄₆₄ in (80 mm) lengths and file a taper on each end. Form a closed scroll on one end; roll it up until a bead resting on it is exactly half way down the length of wire. Planish the scroll.

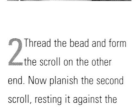

2 Thread the bead and form the scroll on the other end. Now planish the second scroll, resting it against the edge of a flat stake.

3 When all ten links are complete, polish them and bend each scroll downward. Make sure that the planished face is uppermost. Use the remaining wire and the dowel to make jump rings (see page 121) and assemble the units into a chain with the bolt ring on the end. As there are ten units, there will be enough units for the bolt ring to be fastened to one or two units short of the end to leave one or more hanging.

GLOSSARY

ABRADING The wearing away of material using emery and other abrasives.

ACID PICKLE A solution of sulfuric acid, usually about five parts water to one part acid, used to clean metal after soldering. The mixture is best used warm and will remove oxides and spent flux.

ACRYLIC A thermoplastic material that becomes plastic, or softens, when heated. It is available in a wide range of colors, translucent and opaque, as well as clear.

ALLOY A mixture of two or more metals.

ANNEALING The process of softening metals using heat. Most non-ferrous metals can be softened by heating them to dull red and allowing them to cool.

BASE METAL Non-precious metal such as aluminum, brass, copper, gilding metal, nickel, pewter, and steel.

BEARER The narrow shelf inside a bezel upon which a cabochon or other stone rests.

BEARER WIRE Wire that is L-shaped in cross section. It is used to incorporate both bearer and bezel.

BENDING JIG A piece of metal with holes, into which pins are placed. A jig is used to bend wire into different shapes.

BEVEL Slant or inclination of a surface.

BEZEL The narrow strip of metal that is used to secure a stone or cabochon in place.

BINDING WIRE Usually made of soft iron, binding wire is used to fasten work together during soldering.

BLOCKING In repoussé, the work which is done on the back of the metal.

BODKIN A tapered steel tool, rather like a thick blunt needle, and having a wooden handle.

BRASS An alloy of copper and zinc. It is usually yellow in color.

BRONZE An alloy of copper and tin, usually with additions of zinc, lead, and other elements.

BURNISHER A highly polished tool of hardened steel or agate which is rubbed against softer metal to harden it and also to impart a polish.

BURR A rough edge created by filing or drilling metal. This must be removed with care to avoid scratching the surrounding area.

CABOCHON A ground and polished unfaceted semi precious stone, usually round or oval in shape.

CASTING The pouring of molten metal into a mold.

CENTER DRILL A specialized drill with a 60-degree angled section and a narrow tip.

CENTER PUNCH A pointed punch used to make an indent in metal prior to drilling.

CHASING The decoration of metal using punches, working from one side of the metal only. When the metal is worked on from both sides, this is called repoussé.

CHENIER Fine metal tubing, useful for making findings and hinges.

COPING SAW Frame saw slightly larger than a piercing saw, used for sawing curves in wood and for sawing acrylic.

COPPER A reddish non-ferrous metal both malleable and ductile. All metals used in jewelry-making contain some copper.

COUNTERSINK To open out the top of a hole to an angle of 90 degrees, usually to receive a countersunk screw.

DATUM EDGE A straight true edge against which marking out tools such as dividers or a try square can be used when marking out sheet metal.

DIVIDERS Two pointers hinged like a pair of compasses with an adjusting screw. Dividers are used for scribing arcs and for scribing a line parallel to an edge.

DOMING BLOCK A block of brass or steel with hemispherical depressions, used to make domes.

DRAW FILING A method of smoothing an edge by drawing the file along the work at right angles to it.

DRAWPLATE A hardened steel plate comprising a series of tapered holes of diminishing size through which wire is pulled to transform the wire's shape.

DUCTILITY The property of metal that makes it capable of being drawn into wire. Most non-ferrous metals are ductile with the notable exception of lead.

EMERY A coarse rock of corundum and magnetite or haematite used for polishing metal or other hard materials.

EMERY BOARDS Strips of thin wood or board coated with emery or other abrasive. Made with different grades of abrasive, the boards are used for the smoothing of metal prior to polishing.

EMERY PAPER or **CLOTH** Paper or cloth covered with emery, used for polishing.

ETCHING The creation of surface texture and pattern on metal using acids or salts. An acid resist is used to draw a design on the work piece. This is then immersed in the etchant, which erodes the metal where it is left exposed.

FACET A flat surface, one of several, which has been ground and polished on a gemstone or similar.

FERRIC CHLORIDE A chemical used to etch shapes into metal.

FERROUS METALS Metals that consist mainly of iron.

FINDINGS Fixings such as clasps, pins, and earring wires. In former times a jeweler would "find" the metal for the making of these from among metal scraps.

FIRESTAIN A surface film caused by oxidization that remains on sterling silver after heating. Firestain can be prevented by the use of flux or must be removed by abrading and polishing.

FLUX The generic term used to describe a chemical used as an antioxidant during soldering. It works by forming a protective coating between flame and metal, so preventing the formation of oxide and allowing the solder to flow.

FORGING The process of shaping metal using hammers and other tools to the point where the metal's shape is changed substantially. Iron and steel must be forged at red heat but silver and other non-ferrous metals can be forged cold.

FORMER A term used to describe any tool or object that is used to shape metal, including doming blocks, swage blocks, and mandrels.

FORMING The process of changing the shape of metal using formers without altering the metal's thickness.

FUSING The joining of metals by means of heat without the use of solder. The metals being joined melt but only on the surface.

GILBOWS Heavy-duty shears with thick blades.

GILDING METAL An alloy of copper and zinc. Its color ressembles that of gold.

HARDBOARD A thin, even-textured manufactured board, used as a vise guard or drilling base.

JOIN A term used to describe the meeting of two or more pieces of metal for soldering.

JUMP RING A small plain ring used for connecting links in a chain or for hanging pendants from wires or chains.

LAMINATE Layers of material that are sandwiched together.

LEADER A gradual taper filed on the end of wire.

MALLEABILITY The quality of metal that makes it capable of being hammered or rolled permanently out of shape, without breaking or cracking. Most non-ferrous metals are malleable, gold being the most malleable metal of all.

MANDREL A tapered rod, usually with a circular cross-section, used for shaping or stretching rings.

MATTING In repoussé, the process of creating texture on the front of the metal work using punches.

NICKEL SILVER An alloy of copper and nickel, also usually containing some zinc. It is silver in color.

OXIDIZING FLAME A flame with a high proportion of air in it. Used where greater heat is needed, the oxidizing flame leads to more oxide forming on the metal.

PALLION Term for tiny pieces of solder.

PEWTER An alloy of tin, antimony, and copper. Old pewter contains some lead.

PLANISHING The hammering of metal with polished or textured hammers to even out or enliven the metal surface.

POP RIVET A tubular fixing device used by sheet metal workers.

PUNCH AND DIE A tool for making holes in sheet metal. The metal is supported in the die, and the punch is forced through it with a shearing action.

PUSHER A small metal tool used in stone setting. It is usually rectangular in cross-section with a wooden handle.

REDUCING FLAME Contains less air than the oxidizing flame and therefore produces less oxide. It is used for annealing.

REPOUSSÉ The modeling of sheet metal using hammers and punches. The metal is fixed to a yielding surface and work is carried out on both back and front.

RING HOLDER A specialized holding device with a hollow end that can be opened out by means of a screw to grip the ring from the inside.

ROLLING MILL A tool used to reduce the thickness of sheets of metal. Smooth steel rollers encased in a cast iron frame reduce thickness, a little at a time, with each reduction of the gap between the rollers.

ROUGE A polishing compound, the finest and last to be used in the polishing process.

SHANK The back, or reverse, of a ring, away from the setting.

SHEARS Cutting tools for sheet metal, with a similar action to that of scissors.

SOLDERING The joining of metals by means of heat, using silver-based alloys.

SPRUE A passage through which molten metal or wax can be poured into a mold.

STAKES Polished metal formers used by the jewelry maker to support the work being planished or forged. The careful maintenance of stakes, as well as hammers is most important as marks and scratches will be transferred to the work.

STERLING SILVER Also called standard silver, sterling silver is the usual form of the metal used by the jewelry maker. It is an alloy of silver, 92.5%, and copper, 7.5%.

STOPPING OUT The application of an acid resistant medium to a piece of work to be etched.

SWAGE BLOCK A block of steel or wood with rounded grooves of varying sizes, used with rods in the making of chenier.

TRIPOLI A medium-grade polishing compound.

TRY SQUARE An instrument used for marking a line at right angles to an edge or for trying or testing an edge for squareness.

VISE A device for holding work securely while sawing or filing. The squeezing force can be applied with a screw or a wedge.

WIRE DRAWING Making wire thinner, or changing its cross section, by pulling it through successively smaller holes in a drawplate.

WORK HARDENING The process by which metal becomes harder and more brittle as it is repeatedly bent, hammered, rolled, or twisted.

ZINC A white metal mainly used as a constituent of brass and other alloys.

INDEX

All photographs and illustrations are the
copyright of Quarto Publishing plc.